yOur Sense Of HUmOr

Don't Leave Home Without It

K.B. CHANDRA RAJ

Order this book online at www.trafford.com
or email orders@trafford.com

Most Trafford titles are also available at major online book retailers.

Printed in the United States of America.

ISBN: 978-1-4669-5364-2 (hc)
ISBN: 978-1-4669-5362-8 (sc)
ISBN: 978-1-4669-5363-5 (e)

Library of Congress Control Number: 2012915038

Trafford rev. 09/11/2012

 www.trafford.com

North America & International
toll-free: 1 888 232 4444 (USA & Canada)
phone: 250 383 6864 ♦ fax: 812 355 4082

Dedication

When my career arrived at a cul-de-sac in a foreign land, Chels and Maha, by their sterling reputation among the natives for their integrity and intellect, found a way for me to proceed with honor.

A sense of humor was sword and shield for these kindred souls, their families and mine would Friday nights, exchange badinage, bandy jokes, swap shaggy-dog stories, and *find solutions to problems of ethnic discord, world hunger, and the ailing economies of the third world.*

This book is dedicated with love to Chels and Maha, who live in our memories.

Rest well sweet friends. Rest well.

Drum Major for Sense of Humor

"If I had no sense of humor, I would long ago have committed suicide."

—Mahatma Gandhi

Gandhi, Winston Churchill's "half-naked fakir," *won independence for India* from the British, the foremost power at that time. Great Britain during this period held sway over a population of 458 million and had freehold possession of almost one quarter of the global real estate.

Gandhi won independence for India *without firing a single shot.* He did it with that inexhaustible and, to the world, inexplicably awesome firepower of a single philosophy, ironically—*nonviolence* known as ahimsa.

What You Will Find between the Covers

Acknowledgments, Admissions, Admonishments

How I Came to Write This Book

Title

In Praise of Humor: *Laughter Is No Laughing Matter*

Where Can I Find Humor?

Putting Humor to Work

Just Kidding

Situational Irony (Inspired by O. Henry's Masterpiece—"The Gift of the Magi")

I have now come to the end, having labored like a bricklayer piling brick upon brick, and now stand back with satisfaction and (can I say it?) pride to view the end product. One line after another until it has now filled up from the bottom, like a barrel of apples. As to how readers will react, I do not know just yet, for reactions of individuals are always inevitably subjective as they are captive to predilections and cultural backgrounds, tastes and habits, gender and generation which keep evolving. Yesterday's proud peacock is sadly today's feather duster.

Acknowledgments

Thanks once again to my loving wife Siva, who can be depended upon to quarterback every project successfully to the end zone; always eager to afford me the time, succor, and safe harbor to pursue my goals, she never seemed to tire of asking me with genuine affection, how the book was progressing.

Thanks to the librarian, Maureen Armstrong, and her amiable and able assistants at the Whitneyville branch of the Hamden Public Library, who reach beyond the grasp to assist patrons and help create an environment conducive to research and writing. For over eight years, like T. S. Eliot's Alfred Prufrock, I have at this library where a preponderance of the work was done, measured out my life most mornings and afternoons, not with "coffee spoons" as Prufrock did but in library hours.

Thanks to my family and close friends in the United States and abroad for their words of encouragement following my publication *For the Love of Shakespeare*.

Thanks to my childhood friend and muse Dr. R.S. Perinbanayagam for his wise counsel through out this project.

Thanks to the genial and openhanded Andrea Grimes, special collections librarian at the San Francisco Public Library, for providing me with copies of Nat Schmulowitz's stellar catalogues on wit and humor, which have the well-deserved reputation of being the best in the world.

Admission

> This book is not meant to be a *magnum opus* and overly scholarly.

Some of what you will find here may have strayed into my domain just as innocently as baby Eppie did into the heart and home of Silas Marner, changing his miserly miserable life of counting gold coins into a man with a loving heart of gold.

I realize that a book on humor must contain much more than what you will find here. The omission can be explained: for reasons of sheer physical and logistical constraints, it is not possible to include everything. It is not possible to please everybody.

This book is designed to amuse, but we all know that a diet of uninterrupted merriment soon palls. Even kids want to get off the Ferris wheel after a while.

Cartoons need fuller-size display format, and performance humor needs an actor, scenery, and a stage. I have, to the best of my ability, confined jokes, anecdotes, and the like that can come to life in the printed page.

Any errors in fact, interpretation, or awareness are entirely mine; editing was all mine too—self-editing like administering colonoscopy to oneself can be somewhat tricky, although, believe it or not, Yugoslav-born plastic surgeon Dimitrije Panfilov performed liposuction on himself to remove a double chin.

Admonition

Let your speech always be with grace, seasoned as it were, with salt, so that you may know how you should respond to each person. (Apostle Paul)

If therefore you have that insurmountable urge to poke fun, if you really must, then I say poke fun at those who have become insufferable because of an oversized ego. Poking fun at the weak, as late night comedians do for ratings, ridiculing and diminishing those who need medical treatment by dehumanizing and trivializing their sickness with derisive laughter is nothing short of shameless bullying or schadenfreude. We should not laugh at the natural defects of anyone who has no way of remedying them. It's crass cruelty to clobber a cripple with his own crutches. In a coliseum, what is sport to one is death to another. Say nothing that would bring the blush of shame to the cheek of the reader. You can be biting, robust, and colorful but never salacious. Aim your derision at the quality of weakness, not at a weak person. Be funny, not filthy. Denounce human frailty, not human being. Laugh with yourself, laugh at yourself, and laugh with others. Laughter should be capable of reciprocity. It should not flow in one direction. It's worth noting in this context what was said of the great satirist, Dr. Swift, the author of *Gulliver's Travels*: "He lashed the vice but spared the name . . . He spar'd a hump or crooked nose . . . True genuine dullness moved his pity, unless it offered to be witty." We must remember not to fight fire with fire. Water does a better job!

Shakespeare provides us with two models—Falstaff and Iago. While Falstaff shamelessly breaks all moral laws, he is not mean, and he is not malicious, whereas Iago is the personification of cunningness and cruelty which results in tragedy.

I have by design avoided bawdy lyric, those of fully fledged four-letter variety and ethnic put-down jokes that titillate some and tease the others.

Selection

How did I select what appears in this book? By instinct rather than rule—each person's sense of humor is unique as his or her thumbprint.

Suggestion

I suggest you read straight through, for there is continuity in chapters—first to the final. Thereafter, you may use this book as a coaster, to right a wobbly table, in lieu of a hammer, a flyswatter, an umbrella, and a fan. Ladies may use it to balance on their heads to improve their posture or as John Grisham by his own admission actually did with his unsalable "A Time to Kill"—as a doorstopper.

Adjuration

Please reserve your objurgations, execrations, hoots, jeers, catcalls, and cavil until you have read the last line of the last chapter.

Admiration

We must all admire the humility of Leonardo di ser Piero da Vinci who gave the world the *Mona Lisa*, the most famous and most parodied portrait, and *The Last Supper*, the most reproduced religious painting of all time.

In our meanderings through life's thicket, in our struggles, and in our search for credibility and excellence, may the words of this genius, a giant by any measure, be our GPS.

I have offended God and mankind because my work did not reach the quality it should have. (Leonardo di ser Piero da Vinci)

K.B. Chandra Raj
September 16, 2012.

How I Came to Write This Book

Most people read. It could be the train schedule, do-it-yourself manuals, romantic novels by Nora Roberts and Nicholas Sparks, biographies by Walter Isaacson and Doris Kearns Goodwin, thrillers by John Grisham, or a classic like *Grapes of Wrath* by John Steinbeck. So much for those who read; how about writers? I have always wondered what moves writers to write and how they choose their subject. Mr. Grisham's forensic thrillers come out of the press quicker than a yellow traffic light can change to red; Steve Jobs wanted his children to know about him and so assigned the writing of his biography to that talented writer, Walter Isaacson. Ms. Goodwin's well-acclaimed *Team of Rivals* on Lincoln surely involved intensive research. Did Ms. Goodwin feel there is more in Lincoln's life the world needed to know and therefore undertook her *Team of Rivals*? I would think so, for writing about Lyndon Johnson and the Kennedys, she says, "I already knew something about the subjects and was curious to know more." We know John Steinbeck felt deeply and was moved by the sorry plight of California farmers which gave the world the classic *Grapes of Wrath*; and in the case of Ernest Hemingway, was it an excuse to get himself a new bride? F. Scott Fitzgerald had noted that Hemingway needed a new wife for every new book. Mitch Albom who has written good fiction once stated that he would not write unless he felt moved by the theme and could do justice expressing it. William Falkner was forthright. When asked why he wrote, with characteristic Irish candor, replied, "For money of course."

Like a play is not realized until it is acted and the fullness of a music composition is heard only in performance, so too a book is not written unless it is read.

An author can only hope in this day of twenty-four-hour television, breaking news (real and manufactured [sharks in Florida, missing persons in the Midwest]), Internet, e-mail, Facebook, Twitter, texting, Howard Stern; Rush Limbaugh, Don Imus, the malapropisms of Sarah Palin, the (oops) misstatements of Michele Bachmann (want more?), Match.com, Ok Cupid, and eHarmony.com that people will find the time to read his book.

To those therefore who have the discipline and fortitude to dis the above "distractions" and read this book I am truly beholden.

Encouraged by the words of Rabelais, the foremost laugh-raiser that ever lived, "Tis better to write of laughter than of tears; since laughter is the property of man." Let's begin.

This was no run-of-the-mill humdrum "What do you expect—this is New England" kind of year—the winter of 2010. Newscasters who have a penchant for hyperbole and a predilection for labeling like "king of pop," "the hammer," and "queen of mean" branded it "snowmageddon."

To children, snow brings double joy—sledding outdoors and early closing or no school at all. As adults, they could cope, a little inconvenience maybe, and now as elders or vintage persons I would prefer to describe them they felt this year they have had enough. When snow piles up eight to nine inches at the entrance to the apartment, I would not describe it as Dickens did, "the best of times." "I am moving to Florida" chant this time had a new zing to it. It is pretty clear that they were not aware of the prevailing stand-your-ground law of Florida, where you could kill an unarmed person if you felt your life was in danger. And I asked myself, "Haven't I seen this movie before?" Don't you worry, come next year, they will all be right here. I am a "tropical animal." I am resigned to, even grown to accept the celestial confetti but this. An avalanche descending upon us with absolutely no signs of letting! Chione (the goddess of snow) has turned choleric. She was using both hands and feet to maul us. The only ones smiling were the snowplow operators, and they rolled in, in their pickup-like tanks, as though to liberate a village held hostage.

However nasty and brutish the weather may be, with adamantine inflexibility, Sisyphean regularity, and an idée fixe of sorts, I would keep my trysts with the gym and the library. So willingly would I supplicate myself with native humility to these twin earthly gods of mine that it surely must make even the demure Thulasi, the Hindu goddess of fidelity blush with envy. I had two urgent letters that had to catch the next day's mail. I drove up to the post office after my daily regimen at the library. Gray evening had turned creepy dark, and the cold was getting to the old bones. I parked the car as close as possible to the mailbox mindful of the law, and with the heater full blast, I made a dash for it. There were two others ahead of me—a lady and then a gentleman.

As soon as the lady dropped her letter in the mailbox and turned to leave, the gentleman remarked, "My letter will get to the destination before yours." She looked back with a smile. "You think so! Good luck." So saying, she hurriedly left. Mind you, this was between two strangers on a very cold night. For a brief moment, she forgot the cold, and I was amused.

My wife and I took our seats on *Delta Air Lines* strapped for San Francisco. I lazily looked at the harried passengers boarding, to whom going through security was always a harrowing experience—handing over everything you own as though you are on your final journey to meet your maker. You might as well travel dressed in a shroud. I was making a mental note of the size of their carry-on luggage and of women's "purses," which when flying nowadays turn not into pumpkins but catchall contraptions. An elderly gentleman, accompanied by his wife, sashayed between the aisles, wheeling his luggage and paused at the seat assigned to him. He, wobbly though, managed to lug the carry-on up to his neck but was unable to heave it into the overhead cabin. A youngster sprang to his feet and with casual ease placed it into the cabin and click-closed it. Touched by the youngster's kindness and holding him gently by the shoulder, he thanked him and remarked mischievously, "Son, what took you so long?" The two exchanged smiles.

The captain addressed the passengers. The customary welcome, the weather in San Francisco, the altitude at which we will be flying, and then this: "Passengers are cautioned not to disable the smoke detector or tamper with any equipment on the aircraft. The penalty for any such infraction is a two-thousand-dollar fine. Now if you can afford that kind of money," he said, "you should be flying *American.*" Passengers chuckled.

I was on the Metro-North commuter train, returning one evening from New York City and approaching my destination—New Haven. The conductor, a white gentleman, was walking toward the vestibule. He saw two African American middle-aged women. (One was holding a bicycle.) He stopped and talked. The three of them engaged in pleasant banter and were now smiling—the smiles blossomed into subdued laughter, and then a happy threesome tête-à-tête ensued. From snatches of the conversation I could catch, one holding the bicycle was recounting the close calls she has had cycling on the road. The conductor left; the smiles on the faces of the women lingered. What I witnessed warmed my heart. Here was an official who dealt with men, women, (at times) bawling babies, and those handicapped and hard of hearing all day every day and, at the tired tail end of a strenuous day's work, still retained his *sense of humor* and a feeling of camaraderie. I will never be able to recognize this gentleman even if he came within slapping distance of me, but I will remember respectfully the attitude he brought to bear to his work. He took with him to work his *sense of humor* and was now with it, as Thomas Gray noted, he "Hies home at evenings close; to sweet repast and calm repose."

It became clear to me that it must make one feel good and make others feel good by just being good-naturedly flippant and funny. I decided to be "flippant and funny." You'll see how it turned out.

(At this point I must digress. Those who were born and raised in the United States—unlike me the writer, a citizen by choice and not chance—whose progenitors reach back several generations and whose peregrinations have been confined to the borders of this country are likely to call the above episodes "big deal." I have lived and worked for long periods in three continents, and having travelled widely, I can say with conviction [I have no axe to grind and no intentions of running for Congress], Big deal? *Yes! Big deal!* Americans are more engaging than their counterparts in other countries. They will have you smile than be surly. They welcome the challenge of a friendly civilized banter to a boorish standoff and a warm hug to a cold handshake. Big deal indeed!)

Now for my foray into being funny.

It is my custom to frequent this restaurant for my favorite combo-turkey sandwich and a bowl of broccoli cheddar soup. There were four customers ahead of me. I noted the girl at the register take the orders and discharge them efficiently without once looking up. It was my turn now. I glance back. There were four or five persons behind me. The girl continued to stare at the register.

"What would you have?" she asked, looking into the register.

"Turkey sandwich and a bowl of broccoli cheddar soup please."

"Chips or bread?" she asked, looking into the register.

"Chips."

"To go or to stay?" still looking into the register.

"To go."

"Your name?" still looking into the register.

"Ugly face!"

"Could you spell it for me?"

"U-G-L-Y."

She looked right into my face and said, "Oh my god! I almost punched it in" and then got into a giggling fit and turned to a colleague close by with that "You won't believe this. Wait till I tell you" look. She still doesn't know my name, never asks for it, and now takes my order with a smile as though there exists between us a covenant.

There must surely be more to humor than just soup and sandwich I surmised. I decided to learn more. In yore, yore days if I was a seeker of knowledge like those of my ilk and heritage, I would have had to trek through the jungle for many days to a guru venerated for his wisdom, piety, and mental acuity, (what wafts through my mind like a cool breeze during the enervating heat of summer is the name Swami Sri Ramana Maharishi, sage of Arunachala in Tamil Nadu) sit at his feet and attend on him hand and foot with diligence and devotion. If he was convinced that

I was an earnest seeker, he would then take me on as his *sishya* (student) and impart to me the knowledge he had acquired by meditation and divine inspiration. I am dumb enough to know no divine inspiration is likely to descend on me anytime soon. We have come a long way. I decided to consult the modern-day guru, the Google, about humor from within the comfortable confines of my home.

Blistering Barnacles! The screen lit up with titles of books by prominent authors. *Jesus Laughed: The Redemptive Power of Humor* by Robert Darden, *The Joke and Its Relation to the Unconscious* by Sigmund Freud, *Enjoyment of Laughter* by Max Eastman, *American Tall Tales* by Pope Osborne, *Shakespeare and the Uses of Comedy* by J. A. Byrant Jr., *Humor: Its Origin and Development* by Paul E. McGhee, *Anatomy of An Illness* by Norman Cousins, *Laughter in Hell: The Use of Humor during the Holocaust* by Steve Lipman, and on and on a long list.

I found that however many books I may read, there is more to read. Our view and attitude on any subject is akin to the three blind men who offered varying descriptions of an elephant, depending on which part of the animal's body they came into contact with.

My mother's kitchen like New York City never sleeps. She would say rhetorically that at some point one must stop cooking and start eating. With that gleeful impatience of a mosquito in a nudist colony anxious to get as many bites as possible before she or he is slapped and sent to nirvana, I underlined, sidelined, highlighted, made marginal comments (chuckling all the while) by my last count ninety-six books, put them away, retrieved them, and reread them along with the clippings I had collected over the years on related topics. Now, these books have the "fingerprint evidence" of well-used books—curled corners, wrinkled spines, creases, cross-references, and annotations. Samuel Johnson said it best: "The greatest part of a writer's time is spent in reading in order to write. A man will turn over half a library to make a book." I decided that now it's time to stop reading and start writing.

What you will find in this book is the essence (without pulp) and the quintessential wit and wisdom of my research.

The aim of this book is to make the reader laugh. So pray, do not pause to ponder, pinch, and poke to check whether the fruit is ripe but rather read the book with a smile and a song in your heart, in the laziest and self-indulgent manner; read it with feet on the sofa or in couchant position, peanuts or popcorn within reach, unconcerned of the constant back ground hum of the television, Pandora's music from every room, or the sweet prattle of children. Let's not frit away God's gift of laughter, so laugh like pygmies if you like, like children, like Zorba the Greek, get goose flesh, allow the hairs on your neck to head north, lie on the ground and kick your legs in the air (panting and shaking in paroxysms of laughter). Care not what other people think when you laugh out loud. *Have fun!*

A cautionary note: Anthony Trollope died of excessive laughter occasioned by readings from F. Anstey's comic novel, *Vice Versa*, and it is believed the ancient Greek painter Zeuxis, reacting to the portrait of a hag he had just completed, died laughing. So watch out.

There is a myriad of theories about humor. Among them, three are well known: (a) *the superiority theory*—when Jay Leno laughs at Arnold Schwarzenegger's accent, (b) *the incongruity theory*—"George W. Bush will be remembered as one of the greatest thinkers of our time," and (c) *the relief theory*—the Republican debate in Rochester, Michigan, was tense and eagerly watched. Governor of Texas Rick Perry, a candidate, announced that when he becomes president, he would surely abolish three government agencies. He was able to name two but tried as hard as he did the third-energy (oops) he could not. The other candidates on the stage laughed, the moderator beamed, the audience burst into laughter, and those who watched it on television must have laughed as well. I call the relief theory the *diaper theory*—the relief, although welcome, is temporary.

What do I mean by sense of humor?

Is it initiating jokes, funny anecdotes, puns, and the like?

Is it clowning, acting silly, and witty exchanges?

Is it laughing in the midst of adversity? Is it seeing the comical side in times of tribulation?

It is all the above and the ability and the desire to make your friends and acquaintances feel good. I have therefore extended my reach to grab as much as possible to achieve this goal. You will find satire, irony, comic verses, and much more; everything I felt will make you feel good.

Why a sense of humor is important?

Like a table that needs four sturdy legs for it to stay stable and steady on the floor, we too need four props to keep us sane during turbulent times. *A good sense of humor* is one prop, and the other three are: keeping busy, good friends, and prayer (self-reflection).

What test did I apply in selecting the material you are about to read?

Will children have to be sent out of the room to repeat them? Scatological humor has no place here.

Would one have to get permission from someone present to utter them lest she or he may take offense?

The answer to both the above is a firm *no.*

It's worth mentioning as a cautionary note that when Max Eastman mentioned to Bernard Shaw that he was planning to write a book on wit and humor, this was the *encouragement* he received: "There is no more dangerous literary symptom than a temptation to write about wit and humor. It indicated the total loss of both."

As you can see, I have set myself a Promethean task. Promethean task though it may be, neophytes at writing can take comfort and confidence in Will Edwards's "The Impossible Task." Here's how the story goes.

One day a bunch of frogs decided to have a race to see if anyone could get to the top of a tall tree. As the race started, some of the people in the crowd began to comment,

"Oh, they'll never make it."

"That tree is just too tall for a frog to climb."

"They don't have a chance."

Many of the frogs fell back to the ground, but a small group continued the race. The crowd still did not believe they would be able to make it and you could hear them saying:

"They are all going to get hurt."

"They are all way too high."

"This is really dangerous."

And sure enough, the remaining frogs fell from the tree—all but one, that is. He made it all the way to the top, and, when they asked him how he had managed to climb that tall tree, it turned out that . . . the winner was deaf.

If after reading this book, you feel somewhat convinced that there is potential in humor to make your life pleasant, I have accomplished my goal. And that is my wish.

The Title

Your Sense of Humor—Don't Leave Home without It

Often have we heard it said, "Mr. Exxe has a good "sense of humor." We also know that no one likes to be told he does not have a sense of humor. But then there are several kinds of humor: (a) morbid humor—having fun at other people's weaknesses and handicaps, (b) distractive humor—momentary escape from emotional setback while watching the antics of children or watching movies, (c) power humor—psychologically getting on top of the situation by putting the issue or enemy down and, by extension, rising above it, (d) connective humor—connects people to each other and to the tragedy while reminding them that they are bigger than the tragic event, (e) survival humor—as did the Jews during the Holocaust and the blacks during the antebellum period, and (f) dry humor—where the teller of the story does his best to conceal the fact that he even dimly suspects that there is anything funny as in this case for example, "My husband was Irish. I once told him that a man passing me in the street, said to me, 'Hello, gorgeous.' My husband replied with a straight face, 'What color was his guide dog?'"

It is possible to be lost in theories. Almost every major figure in the history of philosophy has proposed a theory.

After twenty-five hundred years of discussion, there has been little accord as to what constitutes humor. There is a plethora of books on humor and definitions abound. This book is intended to make the reader chortle and chuckle. I do not therefore wish to weigh him or her down with soporific definitions.

To condense the whole megillah:

In the sixteenth century, the prime meaning of humor was a "disorder of the blood." However, Hippocrates gave the above nebulous description substance and form with the four elements. A *good sense of humor* is a cocktail of these four elements:

1. Choler or yellow bile representing *anger*
2. Black bile representing *melancholy*
3. Red (blood) producing *cheerful spirit*
4. Phlegm—the cause of *sluggishness*

When these four elements are in harmony (a good cocktail comes to mind), we have a person with a good sense of humor.

All of us can identify humor when we see it. Someone remarks, "Mr. Wye is a humorous person." We get the picture. Then we also hear, "Ms. Whey is very witty." We have a problem. What is the difference? The line of distinction between *wit* and *humor* is friable. Charles S. Bright, even though he admits the distinction is subtle, has done a splendid job of separating the men from the boys, and I quote him verbatim:

> The mouth of a merely witty man is hard and sour until the moment of discharge. Nor is the flash from a witty man always comforting whereas a humorous man radiates a general pleasure and is like another candle in the room. Wit, if it be necessary, uses

its malice to score a point—like a cat it is quick to jump—but humor keeps the peace in an easy chair. Wit is as sharp as a stroke of lightning, whereas humor is diffuse like sunlight. When it tumbles wit is sour, but humor goes uncomplaining without dinner. If a humorous person falls out of a canoe he knows the exquisite jest while his head is still bobbing in the cold water. A witty man, on the contrary, is sour until he is changed and dry: but in a week's time when company is about, he will make a comic story of it.

We need to make an effort to recall the witticisms of Samuel Johnson and Winston Churchill and Wilde's earthy cracks but remember with relish the humor in Orwell's *Animal Farm*, Cervantes' *Don Quixote*, or Toole's *A Confederacy of Dunces*.

In Praise of Humor: *Laughter Is No Laughing Matter*

In this chapter, you will read eminent men and women of letters, philosophers, actors, and entertainers extolling the virtues of humor and laughter. There are exceptions of course—Isaac Newton is reported to have laughed precisely once in his life (when someone asked him what he saw in Euclid's *Elements*) and others whom humorist Rabelais calls agelasts (non-laughers) are notably Jonathan Swift, William Gladstone, Margaret Thatcher, and Supreme Court Justice Ruth Bader Ginsburg. Shakespeare too had met agelasts who refused to "show their teeth in way of smile, though Nestor swear the jest be laughable." Queen Victoria refused to be amused—"Why be happy when you could be *normal*?" Socrates laughed rarely. Well, Spinoza laughed out loud only when watching his favorite sport—that of two spiders fighting to their death. These men and women did not have it in them to laugh and be amused. Alas, what was never joined cannot be separated. All audible laughter for them is ill-bred display and unsightly bodily contortion. Lord Chesterfield congratulates himself that since he has had the full use of his reason; nobody has ever heard him laugh. He went further: In 1748, he wrote to his son "having mentioned laughter, I must particularly warn you against it . . . frequent and loud laughter is the characteristic of folly and ill manners; in my mind there is nothing so illiberal and so ill-bred as audible laughter." Rabelais lumps these non-laughers with certain cannibals and misanthropists. Jesus wept, but did he laugh? The absence of humor from the Bible has fomented spirited discussion. In the Bible, laughter gets a black eye. "Sorrow is better than laughter: for by the sadness of the countenance the heart is made better." And later, "For as the crackling of thorns under a pot, so is the laughter of the fool: this also is vanity." We wonder whether they (the non-laughers) bleed when pricked and yet it is possible too that these illustrious men and women are not humor-impaired but like yogis are perfectly happy, in tune with the universe that they do not find the need for laughter the way the majority does. The early social psychologist McDougall noted, "The perfectly happy man (woman) does not laugh, for he has no need of laughter." Benjamin the donkey in the *Animal Farm* for instance never laughed. If asked why, he would say he saw nothing to laugh about.

Heaven has given us three things to combat—the toilings, moilings, and miseries of this world. Sleep, *laughter* and the hope that things will get better. *Some believe it is cheerfulness not cleanliness that is next to godliness.*

I am confident that once Benjamin begins reading this book, he is going to grin, giggle, chortle, and chirrup all the way to the end.

> Gentlemen, why don't you laugh? With the fearful strain that is upon me night and day, if I did not laugh, I should die. (Abraham Lincoln)

How did Abraham and Sarah react when the Lord tells the ninety-year-old Abraham that they are going to have a child? They fell on their faces and just laughed. For different reasons of course: Abraham happy that he would be blessed with an heir. Sarah too laughed. We do not know whether it was from disbelief or derision. We can all agree it was laughter. They named their only son Isaac, the name in its origin means *he who laughs.*

*Humor is the kiss Joy and Sorrow give each other. (Max Eastman)

*The best of healers is good cheer. (Pindar, the great poet of the fifteenth century BC)

*Love, laughter and living are three great prizes in life. (Robert Holden)

*One laugh of a child will make the holiest day more sacred still. (Robert G. Ingersoll)

*Laughter is higher than all pain. (Elbert Hubbard)

*The key to a healthy marriage is laughter. (Michelle Obama)

*Laughter is the most civilized music in the world. (Peter Ustinov)

*There is nothing in the world as irresistibly contagious as laughter. (Charles Dickens)

*No person who has once heartily and wholly laughed can be altogether irreclaimably bad. (Thomas Carlyle)

*Good humor is one of the best articles of dress one can wear in society. (William Makepeace Thackeray)

*If you can find humor in anything, you can survive it. (Bill Cosby)

*Against the assault of laughter, nothing can stand. (Mark Twain)

*Laughter can be heard farther than weeping. (Yiddish proverb)

*Humor is not a mood, but a way of looking at the world. (Ludwig Wittgenstein)

*Shared laughter creates a bond of friendship. (W. Grant Lee)

*One can know a man from his laugh, and if you like a man's laugh before you know anything of him, you may confidently say that he is a good man. (Fyodor Dostoyevsky)

*Laughter is the shortest distance between two people. (Victor Borge)

*Humor is the instinct for taking pain playfully. (Max Eastman)

*If you want special illumination, look upon the human face; see clearly within laughter the Essence of Ultimate Truth. (Jalaluddin Rumi)

*A person without a sense of humor is like a wagon without springs. It's jolted by every pebble on the road. (Henry Ward Beecher)

*When humor goes, there goes civilization. (Erma Bombeck)

*I think the next best thing to solving a problem is finding some humor in it. (Frank A. Clark)

*You can turn painful situations around through laughter. If you can find humor in anything, even poverty, you can survive it. (Bill Cosby)

*A sense of humor is the ability to understand a joke—and that the joke is oneself. (Clifton Paul Fadiman)

*If you could choose one characteristic that would get you through life, choose a sense of humor. (Jennifer Jones)

*The man who cannot laugh is not only fit for treasons, stratagems and spoils; but his whole life is already a treason and stratagem. (Thomas Carlyle)

*Behind every laugh, there is a story being told. (Robert Holden)

*True humor springs not more from the head than from the heart, it is not contempt, and its essence is love. (Thomas Carlyle)

*You grow up the day you have the first real laugh at yourself. (Ethel Barrymore)

*I am persuaded every time a man smiles, but much more when he laughs; it adds something to his fragment of life. (Laurence Sterne)

*The heart which is not struck by the sweet smiles of an infant is still asleep. (Hazaert Inayat Khan)

*Being silly is not silly, being silly is a first step to being free. (R. Holden)

*We don't laugh because we're happy—we're happy because we laugh. (William James)

*Laughter is the best way to make somebody's heart beat. (R. Holden)

*Humor is an affirmation of dignity, a declaration of man's superiority to all that befalls him. (Romain Gary)

*Laughter is not at all a bad beginning for a friendship, and it is by far the best ending for one. (Oscar Wilde)

*A Good laugh is sunshine in a house. (William Makepeace Thackeray)

*Laughter is worth a hundred groans in any market. (Charles Lamb)

*Laughter is a total body experience in which all the major systems of the body such as the muscles, nerves, heart, brain and digestion participate fully. (Dr. Fry)

*Laugh and the whole world laughs with you. (Ella Wheeler Wilcox)

*Men show their character in nothing more clearly than by what they think laughable. (Goethe, German poet)

*Imagination was given to man to compensate him for what he is not; a sense of humor to console him for what he is. (Francis Bacon)

*I laugh because I must not cry—that's all, that's all. (Abraham Lincoln)

*Laughter is after speech, the chief thing that holds society together. (Max Eastman)

*A smile is the universal welcome, and laughter is a greeting that we may give to an arriving friend. (Max Eastman)

*Humor is something that thrives between man's aspirations and his limitations. There is more logic in humor than in anything else. Because, you see, humor is truth. (Victor Borge)

*Comedian Michael Pritchard equates laughter to changing a baby's diaper. "It doesn't change things permanently but it makes everything OK for a while."

*A smile is a curve that sets everything straight. (Phyllis Diller)

*Laughter is nothing else but sudden glory. (Thomas Hobbs)

*A light heart lives long. (Shakespeare)

*Laughter has a preventive as well as curative value in regard to health and illness; and studies have shown that laughter aids digestion and stimulates the endocrinological system . . . (American Medical Association)

*Laughter is a form of internal jogging. (Norman Cousins)

*We're all here for a spell; get all the good laughs you can. (Abe Burrows)

*The British: Where would we be without a sense of humor? Germany. (Rosemarie Jarski)

*Those who try to live by Work alone, without Laughter or Prayer turn into insane lovers of power, tyrants who would enslave Nature to their immediate desires—an attempt which can only end in utter catastrophe, ship wreck on the Isle of Sirens. (W. H. Auden)

*To be able to make people laugh is the nicest thing you can do for somebody. (Victoria Wood)

*If only Hitler had a few good one-liners up his sleeve, the course of history might have been different. (Rosemarie Jarski)

*For what do we live, but to make sport for our neighbors and laugh at them in our turn? (Jane Austen)

*Developing a wholesome sense of humor involves laughing with your-self, at your-self, and with others. Let's laugh in our homes, on the job, and at school. We desperately need wholesome laughter. A good sense of humor may indeed be the best sense of all. (Tal D. Bonham)

*When people laugh together, they cease to be young and old, masters and pupils, worker and driver. They have become a single group of human beings enjoying their existence together. (W. Grant Lee)

*When the heart in the body is torn,

Torn and bleeding and broken,

We still have laughter beautiful and shrill. (Heine)

*I have yet to come across a person who will admit to not having a sense of humor. (Mark Twain.)

If humor and laughter and good fun can be so beneficial to a person, the question that must follow is, where can I find it?

The chapter "Where Can I Find Humor?" attempts to provide the answer.

Where Can I Find Humor?

Tongues in trees, books in running brooks, sermons in stones and good in everything.

—William Shakespeare

You can find humor in the nightclub where Don Rickles performs, in television like *Saturday Night Live* where Dana Carvey thrills the viewers by his mimicry of President H. W. Bush; in the movies of Bob Hope, Danny Kaye, Bud Abbott, Lou Costello, or Jim Carey; in the comic strip of Gary Trudeau; in television commercials advertising products—the facial contortions of the Progressive insurance girl, the Aflac-Aflac quacking duck, or the Budweiser Super Bowl commercial watched by millions; and also in the printed *word* if we look for it. Humor is famous for its short shelf life. What convulsed us in the seventies—Archie Bunker in *All in the family*, *The Cosby Show* in the eighties can leave many today cold as being dim, dated, and silly. Humor after all is a reflection of its time—a product of and a comment on society, politics, and customs of the day. Culture, gender, and generation have a great deal to do with it.

What we are concerned here with is mostly the printed word, and there is ample humor in the printed word if only we would look out for it.

In 1962, John Steinbeck that "author within my head" while accepting the Nobel Prize for literature paid obeisance to *the word* by concluding his speech paraphrasing Saint John the Apostle thus: "In the end is the Word, and the Word is Man—and the Word is with Man."

> "Words give wings to the mind and make a man soar to heaven." (Aristophanes)

Aldous Huxley in "Words and Their Meanings."

"Words are magical in the way they affect the minds of those who use them. "A mere matter of words," we say contemptuously, forgetting that words have power to mould men's thinking, to canalize their feeling, to direct their willing and acting. Conduct and character are largely determined by the nature of the words we currently use to discuss ourselves and the world around us."

It is incumbent upon all of us, be she or he, a six-year-old lad or lass in the spring of life, or a sixty-six-year-old senior trundling toward the winter years, when communicating, to choose words with utmost care, for words can hurt and words can heal. I disagree with "Sticks and stones may break my bones but names (words) will never hurt me." The hurt from words take longer to heal. It is an old saying "A blow with a word strikes deeper than a blow with a sword," and words reach where bullets cannot go. Words have consequences. "I give you my word" is a statement that is sacrosanct. While Sarah mocked when she was told she would bear a child, "Let it be to me according to your word," said Mary in humble acceptance when informed of her unlikely pregnancy. "A man of his word" is an honor nonpareil. I may not be prosecuted (successfully) in a court of law for failing to keep my word, but I will certainly be persecuted constantly in the prison of my conscience. Words can give us a great deal of happiness. They can make us smile. They make us feel good. They give us uncontrollable belly chuckles that we hope never end. There is so much goodness in words. Every word has a story. In that delightful, popular cowboy song "A Home on the Range," he longs for "a home where the buffalos roam; where the deer and antelope play," and ah "where seldom is heard a discouraging word . . ."

We can have fun with words by trapping an interlocutor in his own words, making him say the opposite of what he thinks as in this case. "Gambling in stocks is very risky," says a friend, "because you win one day and lose the next." To which, his friend retorts, "Then I'll gamble only every other day." Words can be used as a mechanism with reversible parts. An angry neighbor complains, "What do you mean by emptying your pipe on my terrace?" And the neighbor turns the complaint on its head by asking, "What do you mean by putting your terrace under my pipe?" Children hear words in one circumstance and pretending to be adults repeat them with comic effect. The child hears her mother conversing in the draper's shop and later applies it at home.

"Won't you give me a kiss?" the mother asks. This is how the child enacts what she has heard. "I haven't the new ones in yet. Haven't you any left over from last night? Only one or two, and they are rather dirty and have holes in them."

Words are like pets, dogs in particular. Be nice to them and they will sit, lie, stay, fetch, and follow you everywhere. Exercise them (by selective reading) on a leash, and let them know you are the master or else they will drag you into a ditch. For good behavior, reward them with a dog biscuit and for exceptional service, with sardine.

Harvey Weinstein, the producer of many popular movies including *The King's Speech*, said that words constitute "special effects." We now live in the "written world."

There is romance in words, and in this book, you are going to see a great deal of it.

Words have their limitations too. Charles Dickens, who we believed like a ringmaster could whip words to his every bidding confessed, "No words can express the secret agony of my soul." And T. S Eliot in "The Elder Statesman" stated, "I love you to the limits of speech and beyond/It's strange that words are so inadequate/yet, like the asthmatic struggling for breath/So the lover must for words."

Here's what Elie Wiesel said in his *From the Kingdom of Memory*, "It was by probing silence that I began to discover the perils and power of the word. The walk through fiery night—referring to the killing fields of Treblinka and Auschwitz-, 'the silence before and after the selection, the toneless praying of the condemned . . . the shame and suffering, the haunted eyes . . . I thought that I would never be able to speak of them. *All words seemed inadequate, worn, foolish, lifeless, whereas I wanted them to sear.'"*

And this from the dean of comparative religion, the prince of the English language, Dr. Paul Brunton in his "A Hermit in the Himalayas"—"What can one record of that sublime Void into which I seek to penetrate? Words fail me, phrases elude me, where once they tripped nimbly at my command. My thought, alas, dies before it reaches the point of my pen. Let me then prepare to put the pen aside and let the further pages of this journal be written on water. I cannot take the world with me into such private precincts, nor do I care to. Let that curtain of silence fall upon them."

You will see that there is no getting away from the word. One has to get the best out of it.

At this point, I would like to take the reader on a detour so that together we can go on a scenic tour of the English syntax that is out there or shall I say be allowed to accompany the athletic while kayaking in the fizzing currents of language. Words like Darwin's *Homo sapiens* evolve continuously adapting to changing environment.

Old words give way to new. Ophelia in *Hamlet* sings, "By his cockle hat and staff and sandal *shoon* (shoes)." Some words become dinosaurs. "Belike" meant "most likely" and "certs" meant "in truth." "Respectable" word like "fogey" meaning a "veteran" has become one of derision—"he's an old fogey." A portmanteau of "adorable" and "dork" has produced a person of endearing vulnerability "adorkable." Grandchildren tend to refer to their grandparents as "gerries" truncating geriatric—"I'm going to be spending the vacation with my gerries." We have to be mindful of words being attributed to persons who never uttered them. Marie Antoinette did not say, "Let them eat cake." What she said was "Keep them talking" in the misplaced belief that when people stop talking, they become dangerous. The word "woo" is in a comatose state after having given birth to "dating." The same word can have different meanings in different countries. The "elevator" in the United States is "lift" in the United Kingdom. Yoga is good for reducing stress. But practiced in excess can result in your having a "Yogasm." The nature and tone of forbidden words has certainly changed; there was a time when certain words could not be said in front of a girl. Now you can say them but cannot address a girl as "Girl." You can own it. You must carry it always with you and yet you cannot say the word, "vagina" in the Michigan state legislature. Freud coined the term "penis envy," and it tickled men and women so much it had to be incarcerated, and *he the penis* is now referred to by *his* initials PE. The word "nigger" which in antebellum years was common currency is counterfeit today. In fact, the word "nigger" has in the climate of political correctness slithered from one meaning to another. It changed to "darkies" and now to people of color.

The English word is so malleable that the same word can be used to mean different things. Let's take the word "play;" "theater play," "a baseball play," "fair play," "stock-market play," "playing violin," "playing third base," or "playing someone for a sucker." Even the word "funny" is no longer funny. It can mean ominous as in "he's acting funny" or "the car is making a funny noise."

In Victorian times, people avoided mentioning body parts. You will not hear Dad say at the dinner table, "Never mind the thighs darling. I prefer the nice juicy breasts" while chicken is being dished out.

To go to the toilet (universal), to go to the loo (Englishwomen), to have a pee (Englishmen), to go to the bathroom (American), to go to the lav (New Zealand), to sit on the throne (Shakespeare), and the nurses say, "Sir, you haven't emptied your bladder today."

The need to communicate swiftly to save time and sometimes to send out messages speedily unobserved by the boss has given rise to the pandemic use of acronyms, such as *LOL* for *laugh out loud*, *OMG* for *oh my god*, *IRL* for *in real life*, *DWIT* for do whatever it takes, and *GSOH* for good sense of humor. This trend is rather unfortunate, for it has plucked the bloom out of the rose which is the English word.

We have heard it said ad nauseam to the point of boredom that "a picture is worth a thousand words." That is true, but one word can project a thousand pictures. *Lynching* (as in high-tech lynching) brings to mind right away the Clarence Thomas hearings, Anita Hill, and the left and right media frenzy. We don't need to go blow-by-blow into the atrocities—just say *holocaust* and what comes to mind sadly is the six million European Jews and almost equal number of gentiles who were gassed by Hitler. And "back of the bus" is all Rosa Parks.

(The person who could communicate effectively without words is that master of mime, Charlie Chaplin. He with pants baggy, coat tight, hat small, shoes large, and baby tooth brush mustache. That little man forever in a new hurry stumbling on every pebble on his tread, his silent movements are so expressive that it is beyond the need for words to entertain. Unfortunately, for all others, "words" is the only game in town.)

Humor will not come to us. We must go looking for them. It's not "Bring 'em on"; it's "Go get 'em!"

Prophet Mohammed gathered his followers one day and said, "If we pray with unquestioning faith the mountain to which we trek daily for prayer will come to us." They prayed long and hard, their incantations stretching from sunrise to sunset and from darkness to dawn and yet nothing happened. The mountain remained unmoved. It's the same with humor. Like the mountain and Mohammed, we must go to it, and like the mountain, it's certain to be there and will happily receive us. There's so much out there.

There's widespread disagreement as to how many kinds of humor exists. What we have here is a sample, a fistful. It is not possible to detail them all. You will find there are several dimensions to humor. Some like onomatopoeia and tongue twisters—they are better read with the ear, for they are audio friendly.

The sources of humor you will find here have been broadly categorized. The line of demarcation between categories is frangible, for instance, between boners, witty metaphors, anecdotes, attack and counterattack and the like. Socrates for instance gave a name (irony) to an entire class of humor.

Humor in Fareed Zackaria plagiarism pother or "Schadenfareed"

"Fareed Zackaria, the CNN and Time journalist included a passage in a column on gun control similar to a passage by Jill Lepore in the New Yorker."

And then there was ballyhoo in the media bazar, sanctimonious handwringing and self-righteous flagellation by the Fourth Estate.

There is ample humor in this kerfuffle when viewed against this backdrop.

*Swinburne stole from Keats and Brahms used a theme from Beethoven's ninth for his First Symphony.

("We all work off each other" E.L.Doctorow, author of "Ragtime")

*The title, "Gone with the Wind" comes from an Ernest Dowson Goethe poem.

*The title of Ken Kesey's popular novel, "One Flew over the Cuckoo's Nest" was lifted from the children's folklore, " . . . . one flew East one flew West, **"One flew over the Cuckoo's nest."**

*The book that spurred Gandhi on to embrace the peaceful resistance movement against the British was Tolstoy's controversial (in Russia) book, "The kingdom of God is within you." This title was taken from Luke 17:21 – "Neither shall they say, Lo here, or lo there! For, behold, the kingdom of God is within you." (King James Bible, Cambridge Ed.)

*The title of this book, "Your sense of humor – Don't leave home without it.", filched from "American Express card – Don't leave home without it."

("Words make their way in the world without a master, and any one with little cleverness can appropriate them." Deepak Chopra.)

Hayley of "Roots" fame "had apparently helped to material from a novel called The African by Harold Courlander. A British journalist went to Africa to retrace the steps of the clan Kunta Kinte and found that much of what Hayley wrote was based on made-up tales, to phrase it generously. **All of** which in the grand tradition of the man most historians credit with having originated the modern novel, Daniel Defoe. In 1719, Englishmen were convinced that Defoe had really come across the diary of a shipwrecked sailor named Robinson Crusoe, just as a few years later they believed that Richardson's Pamela really was made up of anguished bulletins from a pretty girl living in a house of an aroused and hard-stalking middle-aged lecher." Tom Wolfe, author of "In Our Time."

The legal donnybrook of transatlantic proportions between Dan Brown (American) author of "Da Vinci Code" and Michael Baigent (British) author of "The Holy Blood and The Holy Grail" is too well known to merit repetition.

"Shakespeare like Puccini was a notorious poacher," Lorrie Moore, Professor of English, University of Wisconsin.

*Shakespeare "borrowed" the story for Romeo and Juliet from a fellow English writer, who got it from a French writer who translated the story from a 16th century Italian tale by Luigi da Porta who swore it was based on fact. Charles Lamb on Shakespeare.

In Antony and Cleopatra **Shakespeare incorporated whole sentences from North's Plutarch into his own text.**

"The legend of Hamlet goes back hundreds of years before Shakespeare. The bard apparently took assorted parts of the many stories about Melancholy Dane (who was probably British in the first place) added his own magic, and came up with the play we know. There apparently was such a man and he did live a pretty violent life." Extract from "The Joy of Trivia" by Bernie Smith.

"Well stolen is half-written."

*Referring to his 2006 annual spring address to the Labor party Prime Minister Tony Blair of Britain "has confirmed to friends that he drew "inspiration" for his long-sign off from a favorite passage of John Steinbeck's classic, "The Grapes of Wrath."

"He later admitted he had "borrowed" heavily from a speech from Tom Joad, the central character of Steinbeck's Pulitzer Prize winning novel about the Great Depression."

"Once the poet lets go of his poem (or prose), it is no longer his. It belongs to anyone who wants it. It's a gift."

Tunku Varadarajan, the Malaysian journalist who coined the word "Schadenfareed" referring to the plagiarism McCarthyites explained it with a pinch of realism and reasonableness thus: "So he (Fareed Zackaria) cribbed a little: he read a lot; took notes; things got jumbled."

As stated elsewhere and worth repeating here in context, Dr. Johnson the 18th Century curmudgeon, wit and author remarked, "A man will turn over half a library to make a book" and, Ms. Goodwin the author of the best seller, "Team of Rivals" who too was accused of plagiarism, tells us she had to add a wing to the main house in order to store the books she had acquired for the purpose of writing the biography. Is it any wonder therefore that notes taken from "half a library", passages copied and poured over, put away, picked up, written, rewritten and polished over a long period should get "jumbled." **The "disproportion between the journalistic lapse and the cyclonic castigation" is where the humor in "Schadenfareed" lies**.

We do not call it plagiarism any more. We say previously used prose.

In academia:

Historian Stephen Ambrose "has been criticized for incorporating passages from the works of other authors into many of his books"

In journalism:

In May 2009, New York Times columnist Maureen Dowd was accused of copying an entire sentence from a "Talking Points Memo" blog.

In literature:

In 1999 J.K. Rowling (author of Harry Potter series of books) "was sued by Nancy Stouffer who claimed the former plagiarized material from the latter's short lived literary career.

With apologies to Songwriters: Smith, Clifford/ Storch, Scott Spencer/ Noble Reggie and Singer Ella Fitzgerald.

Shakespeare and Swinburne did it

Defoe and Dowd did it

Let's do it.

"And that's why birds do it

Bees do it

Even educated fleas do it

Let's do it.

In Spain, the best Upper sets do it

Let's do it.

In Sri Lanka

The Tamils in the North do it

The Sinhalese in the South do it

And in Cleveland everyone does it

Let's do it.

The Dutch in good old Amsterdam

By the canal do it

Let's do it.

Not to mention the Greeks

And the grizzly folks in Alaska do it

Let's do it.

In Tonga the tall and the short do it

Indians dancing the "Banga – banga" do it

Let's do it.

Some in Burma

Without means do it

People say in Boston even beans do it

Let's do it.

Sponges they say do it

Oysters down in oyster—bay do it

Let's do it.

Detainees in Guantanamo blind-folded do it

In China Peking ducks do it so ducky

Let's do it.

From Letterman to Leno and

All in between do it

Let's do it.

Cold Cape—Cod clams

Against their wish do it

Even lazy jelly fish do it

Let's do it.

Electric eels (we can hear) do it

In shallow shoals

English soles do it

Elizabeth and Phillip (they say) do it

In "Down Under" the Australians

Playing possum say softly

"Hey mite" and do it

In Canada "off the boat" refugees do it

Goldfish in the privacy of bowls do it

Let's do it.

We shall fight on the seas and oceans

We shall fight on the beaches

We shall fight on the landing grounds

We shall fight in the fields and in the streets

We shall fight in the hills

Said Churchill and did it

Let's do it.

Now if the birds and the bees

And back-scratching monkeys do it

If Men and Women quarrel

And yet can wake up and make up and still do it

If you can believe Camilla and Charles do it

This entire plagiarism brouhaha baby

Is a lot of huff and puff.

So let's all do it and call off the bluff.

Humor in Garbled Utterances

Here's Sarah Palin's gobbledygook, a verbal dislocation response to Matt Lauer's question when she knew the election was lost.

> I had faith that, you know, perhaps when that voter entered that voting booth and closed that curtain that what would kick in for them was, perhaps, a bold step that would have to be taken in casting a vote for us, but having to put a lot of faith in that commitment we tried to articulate that we were the true change agent that would progress this nation.

It reminds us of what Groucho says in *Duck Soup,* "Chicolini here may talk like an idiot and look like an idiot, but don't let that fool you—he really is an idiot."

Chris Hayes of MSNBC

I think it's interesting because I think it is very difficult to talk about the war dead and the fallen without invoking valor, without invoking the words, "heroes" *Um, and, ah, why do I feel so* . . . comfortable, *Uncomfortable,* about the word because it seems to me that it is so rhetorically proximate to justifications for more war. *Um,* and I don't want to obviously desecrate or disrespect memory of anyone that's fallen and obviously there are individual circumstances in which there is genuine, tremendous heroism, *you know,* hail of gunfire, *rescuing fellow soldiers, and things like that.* But it seems to me that we marshal this word in a way that is problematic. *But maybe I'm wrong about that.*

Christine O' Donnell, referring to Republican candidate Mitt Romney, who was being ridiculed for changing positions, remarked, "He has been consistent since he changed his mind."

This tendency to be circumlocutory is not a recent phenomenon. In the later years of Henry James's life, the novelist's style became notoriously convoluted. Once James attempted from his car, in the company of author Edith

Wharton, to inquire of a doddering pedestrian directions to the King's Road:

> "My friend, to put it to you in *two words*, this lady and I have just arrived here from *Slough;* that is to say, to be more strictly accurate, we have recently *passed through* Slough on our way here, having actually motored to Windsor from Rye, which was our point of departure; and the darkness having overtaken us, we should be much obliged if you would tell us where we now are in relation, say, to the High Street, which, as you of course know, leads to the Castle, after leaving on the left hand the turn down to the railway station."

The old man's face was permeated with befuddlement. James continued:

> "*In short* . . . my good man, what I want to put to you in a word is this: supposing we have already (as I have reason to think we have) driven past the turn down to the railway station (which in that case, by the way, would probably not have been on our left hand, but on our right), where are we now in relation to . . ."

At this juncture, James's companion, Edith Wharton, pleaded that he merely ask the way to the King's Road.

> "Ah. The King's Road? Just so! Quite right! Can you, as a matter of fact, my good man, tell us where, in relation to our present position, the King's Road exactly is?"

> "We're in it," said the aged face at the window.

This kind of verbal incontinence is sometimes colloquially called "bee—ess."

Humor in verse: *For Better or for Verse*

This is a helter-skelter collection of *light* humorous verses of other writers which I fancied as being funny. It's being given to you in scatter-shot order.

It's been my observation, over the years, that many avid readers, well-schooled in the English language tends to distance themselves from verse. All is not lost, dear friends. Poetry proliferation is taking place in London as an adjunct show to the 2012 Olympics. International poets converged on London to orate in fifty languages at a festival called Poetry Parnassus with 100,000 of their collected work dropped by helicopter on the venue by the Thames.

In these little verses, I hope to demonstrate that there is a great deal of fun and enjoyment in verse. I have selected verses with a sting, not the deadly sting of a viper but rather that of a mosquito. They are certain to make you chuckle.

Father

My father knows the proper way

The nation should be run

He tells us children every day

Just what should now be done?

He knows the way to fix the trusts

He has a simple plan.

But if the furnace needs repairs

We have to hire a man.

My father in a day or two

Could land big thieves in jail

There's nothing that he cannot do

He knows no word like "fail."

"Our confidence" he would restore

Of that there is no doubt

But if there is a chair to mend

We have to send it out.

All public questions arise

He settles on the spot

He waits not till the tumult dies

But grabs it while it's hot.

In matters of finance he can

Tell congress what to do

But, O, he finds it hard to meet

His bills as they fall due.

It almost makes him sick to read

The things lawmakers say

Why, father's just the man they need

He never goes astray.

All wars he'd very quickly end

As fast as I can write it

But when a neighbor starts a fuss

'Tis mother has to fight it.

In conversation father can

Do many wondrous things.

He's built upon a wiser plan

Than presidents or kings.

He knows the ins and outs of each

And every deep transaction,

We look to him for theories, *but look to Ma for action.*

(Edgar Albert Guest)

My Mom

My mom brought home a violin

So I can learn to play.

She told me if I practiced hard

I'd play it well someday.

Without a single lesson

I tried to play a song.

My fiddle squeaked, my fiddle squawked

The notes came out all wrong.

My little brother fled the room

Mom covered up her ears.

My puppy dog began to howl.

My sister was in tears.

My dad pulled out his wallet

He handed me a ten.

He made me swear I'd never play

That violin again.

(Anonymous)

The Busy Man

If you want a favor done

By some obliging friend

And want a promise, safe and sure

On which you may depend

Don't go to him who always has

Much leisure time to plan

But if you want your favor done

Just ask the busy man.

The man with leisure never has

A moment he can spare

He's always "putting off" until

His friends are in despair.

But he whose every waking hour

Is crowded full of work

Forgets the art of wasting time.

He cannot stop to shirk.

So when you want a favor done

And want it right away

Go to the man who constantly

Works twenty hours a day.

He'll find a moment, sure, somewhere

That has no other use

And help you, while the idle man

Is framing an excuse.

(Anonymous)

O Karma, Dharma, Pudding and Pie

Gimme a break before I die,

Grant me wisdom, will and wit,

Purity, probity, pluck, and grit.

Trustworthy, loyal, helpful, kind

Gimme great abs and steel trap mind,

And forgive, ye gods, some humble advice

These little blessings would suffice

To beget an earthly paradise.

Make the bad people good

And the good people nice

And before our world goes over the brink

Teach the believers how to think.

(Philip Appleman)

Self-Portrait

I gaze into the mirror

And my frustration grows.

Here's a legend in our time

Whom nobody knows.

(Arnold J. Zarett)

"I love a Martini," said Mabel

I only have two at the most.

After three I am under the table

After four, I am under the host.

(Anonymous.)

Why I want to convert.

Wherever the Catholic sun doth shine,

There's always laughter and good red wine.

At least I've always found it so.

Benedicamus Domino ("Let's Bless the Lord.")

Hilaire Belloc.

A Little More

At thirty:

Five hundred guineas I have saved—a rather moderate store.

No matter; I shall be content when

I've a little more.

At forty:

Well, I can count ten thousand now

That's better than before;

And I may well be satisfied when

I've a little more.

At fifty:

Some fifty thousand—pretty well

But I've earned it sore.

However, I shall not complain when

I've a little more.

At sixty:

One hundred thousand—sick and old; ah,

Life is half a bore,

Yet I can be content to live when

I've a little more.

At seventy:

He dies

And to his greedy heirs he leaves a countless store.

His wealth has purchased him a tomb, and very little more.

(Harry Graham)

The rain it raineth on the just

And also on the unjust fella;

But chiefly on the just, because

The unjust steals the just's umbrella.

(Lord Bowen)

Sir, I admit your general rule

That every poet is a fool:

But you yourself may serve to show it

That every fool is not a poet.

(Alexander Pope)

I Still Love You

Nothing's changed,

I still love you

Oh I still love you

Only slightly, only slightly

Less than I used to, my love.

(Anonymous)

Get Up and Go

How do I know my youth has been spent?

Because my get-up-and-go, got up and went.

But in spite of all that, I am able to grin

When I think where my get-up-and-go has been.

Old age is golden; I've heard it said,

But sometimes I wonder as I go to bed

My ears are in a drawer, my teeth in a cup

My eyes on a table until I wake up.

When I was young my slippers were red

I could kick my heels right over my head

When I grew older my slippers were blue

But I could still dance the whole night through.

Now that I am old my slippers are black

I walk to the corner and puff my way back

The reason I know my youth is spent

My get-up-and-go got up and went.

(Peter Seeger)

The Rich Man

The rich man has his motor car,

His county and his town estate,

He smokes a fifty-dollar cigar

And jeers at fate.

He frivols through the live-long day

He knows not poverty her pinch,

His lot seems light, his heart seems gay,

He has a cinch.

Yet though my lamp burns low and dim,

Though I must slave for livelihood—

Think you that I would change with him?

You bet I would.

(Anonymous)

A centipede was happy quite,

Until a frog in fun

Said, "Pray, which legs come after which?"

This raised her mind to such a pitch

She lay distracted in a ditch.

Considering how to run.

(Anonymous.)

If your lips would save from slips

Five things observe with care:

Of whom you speak: to whom you speak,

And how and when and where.

(Anonymous.)

Girls, to this advice give heed

In affairs with men

If at first you don't succeed,

Cry, cry again.

(Anonymous.)

Women's faults are many,

Men have only two:

Everything they say

And everything they do.

(Anonymous.)

Come on in,

The water's fine.

I'll give you

Till I count to nine.

If you are not in by then,

Guess I'll have to

Count to ten.

(Anonymous)

Dieter's Prayer

Lord, won't you help me?

It's that time of year.

Winter has come and gone.

Springtime is here.

Is this season of flesh?

Won't you show that you care?

Lord, won't you heed

This dieter's prayer?

Teach me tonight

To love cottage cheese,

Grape fruit and celery,

Lord, if you please

Make me believe

That tofu's a food,

And not something you made up

When you were in a bad mood.

Lord won't you help me?

Show that you care.

Lord, won't you heed

This dieter's prayer?

Make me believe

That ice cream's just awful.

That the devil's hiding

Inside every waffle.

That mayonnaise is nothing

But a communist plot.

That broccoli is good for you

And chocolate is not.

Keep me away

From the refrigerator door

When life is a trial

And love is a bore.

Save me from nachos,

And tacos and chips.

For what goes in my mouth

Always lands on my hips.

Oh, pizza, oh, pasta,

Oh, popcorn, oh, pork!

Get thee behind me,

Oh, knife and oh, fork.

And chicken fried steak

From the deepest of south

Oh, Lord, if you love me,

Won't you please shut my mouth?

Oh, Lord, do you hear me?

Honk if you're there.

Lord, won't you heed

You know my need.

Oh, Lord, won't you heed

This dieter's prayer?

(Amanda McBroom)

Temporary Song

I'm a temporary worker

With a temporary job,

And my temporary income isn't much,

But I'm happy for the moment

In a temporary way,

And for temporary reasons

That's enough.

I've got temporary colleagues

And a temporary desk,

And temporary duties to fulfill.

My superior she greets me

With a temporary smile

'Cause I only have a temporary skill.

There's nothing wrong with me nine to five,

It's just a way to stay alive.

I'm a temporary worker with a temporary job,

And my temporary money's always spent.

But I'm happy for the moment

In a temporary way
'Cause my temporary income
Pays my temporary rent.
(Julie Gold)

Leave-Taking

The proper way to leave a room
Is not to plunge it into a gloom;
Just make a joke before you go,
And escape before they know.
(Gelett Burgess)

Waste

I had written to Aunt Maud,
Who was on a trip abroad
When I heard she'd died of cramp
Just too late to save the stamp.
(Harry Graham)

A Word to Husbands

To keep your marriage brimming
With love in the loving cup,
Whenever you're wrong, admit it;
Whenever you're right, shut up.
(Ogden Nash)

Susie Lee done fell in love

She planned to marry Joe.

She was so happy 'bout it all

She told her Pappy so.

Pappy told her, "Susie gal

You'll have to find another.

I'd just as soon yo' Ma don't know,

But Joe is yo' half brother"

So Susie put aside her Joe

And planned to marry Will.

But after telling Pappy this,

He said, "There's trouble still.

You can't marry Will, my gal;

And please don't tell your mother,

But Will and Joe and several mo'

I know is yo' half brother."

But Mama knew and said, "My child,

Just do what makes you happy.

Marry Will or marry Joe,

You ain't no kin to pappy."

(Anonymous.)

Time to Move On

Your love is like butter gone rancid.

Your voice is like scratching of chalk.

Whatever first brought us together

Has like totally gone for a walk.

(Tom Mulhern)

On the chest of a barmaid at Yale,

Was tattooed the price of ale.

And on her behind,

For the sake of the blind,

Was the same information in braille.

(Anonymous.)

Bring on the Goddamn Cat

Some Guinness was spilt on the barroom floor.

When the pub was shut for the night,

Out of his hole crept a wee brown mouse,

And stood in the pale moon light,

He lapped up the frothy brew from the floor,

The back on his haunches he sat,

And all night long you could hear him roar,

"Bring on the goddam cat."

(Anonymous.)

Ode to a Dental Hygienist

Hygienist, in your dental chair
I sit without a single care,
Except when tickled by your hair.
I know that when you grab the drills
I need not fear the pain that kills.
You merely make my molars clean
With pumice doped with wintergreen.
So I lean back in calm reflection,
With close-up views of your complexion,
And taste the flavor of your thumbs
While you massage my flabby gums.
To me no woman can be smarter
Than she who scales away my tartar,
And none more fitted for my bride
Than one who knows me from inside.
At least as far as she has gotten
She sees how much of me is rotten.
(Earnest A. Hooton)

Recession Is Coming to Town

It's worthless if you've got shares
It's worthless if you've got bonds
It's safe when you've got cash in hand

So keep cash for goodness sake, *hey*

You'd better watch out

You'd better not cry

You'd better keep cash

I'm telling you why:

Recession is coming to town.

Finance products are confusing

Finance products are so vague

The banks make you bear the cost of risk

So keep out for goodness sake, *oh*

You'd better watch out

You'd better not cry

You'd better keep cash

I'm telling you why:

Recession is coming to town."

(Anonymous)

A bachelor is a cagey guy

And has a load of fun

He sizes all the cuties up

And never Mrs. One.

(Anonymous)

Update on Noah

Noah hung the sign up

One evening after dark

A warning to the animals

No Smoking in My Ark.

At first they thought he's joking,

That silly patriarch,

He surely doesn't mean it,

No smoking in his Ark.

But Noah said, "I sure do.

This ain't no schoolboy lark.

Those are my instructions

No Smoking in my Ark.

I don't mind what else you do

But fags give me the pip.

So just remember, boys and girls,

No smoking in my ship."

The hippo snorted, "Gosh Oh Gee"

And added too, "By heck,

Why can't a fella have a puff

Upon the upper deck?"

Noah then got angry

"You can disembark

For disobeying my orders

And smoking in my Ark."

The hippo didn't mind a bit

Just swam off to his park

And there he smoked and smoked and said,

"Go stuff your ruddy Ark."

So Noah called a meeting

"This reply will not do.

If there's any more of this

Then you can all swim too."

The animals all listened

Birds and bees alike

And thought that they might possibly

Call a general strike.

But slowly common sense came back

"We renounce the baccy bug!

They didn't want a watery grave

If Noah pulled the plug.

Then suddenly the rain stopped

The sun began its arc

"Go smoke away," said Noah

"In that hippo park.

And if you can't stop smoking

Take my advice," said Noah

"Try to see if you can just

Smoke a little sloah."

(Kenneth Bain)

Saved by the Bell

There was I,

Waiting at the church,

Waiting at the church.

When I found he'd left me

In the lurch,

Oh, how it did upset me.

All at once, I got a little note,

Here's the very note.

This is what he wrote.

"I can't get away

To marry you today.

My wife won't let me."

So.

Pick yourself up

Dust yourself down,

And start all over again.

(Anonymous)

Heavenly Father, bless us

And keep us all alive,

There's ten of us to dinner,

And food enough for five.

(Anonymous)

On Canada

Ours is a sovereign nation

Bows to no foreign will

But whenever they cough in Washington

They spit on Parliament Hill.

(Joe Wallace)

I love the girls who don't

I love the girls who do;

But best, the girls who say . . . "I don't.

But may be . . . just for you."

(Anonymous)

Busts and Bosoms

Busts and bosoms have I known

Of various shapes and sizes,

From grievous disappointments

To jubilant surprises.

(Anonymous)

Humor in Anecdote

An anecdote is a short and amusing story about a real incident or person.

*An unidentified woman and Winston Churchill:

"Mr. Churchill, I want you to know I got up at dawn and drove a hundred miles for the unveiling of your bust."

Mr. Churchill: "Madam, I want you to know that I would happily reciprocate the honor."

*Famous lawyer and statesman, Joseph Choate was more than usually busy. But the young man insisted on pushing his way into the advocate's office.

"Take a chair," said Choate gently.

"I," blustered the intruder, without apologizing for the interruption, "I am the son of Bishop Maxwell."

"Oh," said Choate, "Please take two chairs."

*It became a sort of standing challenge to force President Coolidge to talk. One Washington matron frankly told him so at a White House dinner.

"I've made a wager, Mr. President," she said, with a disarming smile. "I've bet that I can make you say at least three words."

"You lose," said Coolidge.

*During his last year in office, Churchill attended an official ceremony. While there, he heard two men behind him whispering, "That's Winston Churchill. They say he is getting senile. They say he should step aside and leave the running of the nation to more dynamic and capable men."

When the ceremony was finished, Churchill turned around and said, "Gentlemen, they also say he is deaf."

*George Bernard Shaw once wrote to Winston Churchill:

Enclosed are two tickets to my new play, which opens Thursday night. Please come *and bring a friend, if you have one.*

Replied Churchill: I am sorry; I have a previous engagement and cannot attend your opening. However, I will come to the *second performance if you have one.*

*Alistair Cooke journalist and longtime BBC *Letter from America* writer, near the end of his long married life was asked the secret of his survival.

"Two reasons," Cooke replied. "Frequent separate holidays and increasing loss of hearing."

*When Diogenes was captured by pirates and sold into slavery, his new master asked him if he had a trade. Diogenes replied that he knew no trade but that of governing men. "I would like," he said, "to be sold to a man who needs a master."

His new owner no fool, put Diogenes immediately to work tutoring his two sons.

*Cicero tells us how his friend Nasica avenged himself upon a gentleman by the name of Ennius, upon whom he had paid a call. He had been informed by the maid that Ennius was not at home, and when it came about that Ennuis called upon him, he stuck his head out of the window and said, "I am not home."

"What are you talking about?" said Ennuis. "Don't I know your voice?"

"Why, you rascal," said Nasica, "I believed your maid when she told me you were not at home, and you won't believe me even when I tell you myself."

*Groucho Marx was once in a hotel lobby when a priest, in his clerical color, rushed over to see the great film comedian. "Thank you, Groucho, for bringing so much joy and laughter into people's lives!" he said.

"Thank you," Groucho replied, "for taking so much joy and laughter out of them."

*A thief excused himself to Demosthenes by saying, "I did not know it was yours."

"But you did know," said the other, "that it was not yours."

*Bion the sophist, seeing an envious man looking very downcast, remarked, "Either some great harm has happened to him or some great luck to his neighbor."

*Philip the Great, in passing sentence on two rogues, ordered one of them to leave Macedonia with all speed and the other to try and catch him.

*Socrates used to say, "The best form of government was that in which the people obey the rulers, and the rulers obey the laws."

*Cato, on observing that statues were being set up in honor of many, remarked, "I would rather people would ask, why is there *not* a statue to Cato, than why there *is*."

*Thearidas, while whetting a sword, was asked if it was sharp. "As sharp as slander," he replied.

*Agesilaus, being asked whether he thought justice or bravery the greater virtue, answered, "There would be no need of bravery if all of us were just."

*Someone, in anger at a discussion, gave Socrates a kick. When surprise was expressed at his bearing it patiently, he said, "If an ass had kicked me, should I have brought it before the magistrate?"

*Someone asked Diogenes at what time of life he had best marry. "If you are young," he replied, "*not yet*. If you are old, *never.*"

*When his friends said to Diogenes, "You are old, do relax a little." He answered, "If I had run the long course in a race, would you have said, "Do slack your pace a little at the end?"

*One day, watching a very bad archer practice, Diogenes sat directly in front of the target. "Hey, what are you sitting there for?"

"So as not to get hit," he replied.

*On another occasion, Diogenes saw the child of a prostitute throwing stones into a crowd. "Careful," he said, "you might hit your father."

*When a lecturer was reading his paper endlessly, Diogenes looked over and saw that the scroll was coming to a large white space with no more writing on it. He turned to the audience and said, "Cheer up, men, there's land in sight."

Humor in Attack and Counterattack

Where a person tries to be cynically smart and the other person returns the favor with a one-two punch with a fine turn of wit.

Men have always relished the delights of verbal hand-to-hand combat, calling a spade a spade with imagination, wit, and style.

In these, you'll see a person being picked on, and the "victim" of the uncalled-for attack retaliates with cutting wit.

*Baker to landlord who has a sore on his finger:

"I suppose you dipped it in your beer."

Landlord: "No, but one of your rolls got under my nail."

*Once after they had not spoken to each other for a long while, they met in a narrow street. It was plain that one would have to step aside to let the other pass.

Randolph held his ground. "I never give way to scoundrels," said he.

Clay stepped aside in the muddy gutter. "I always do."

*Mark Twain and Paul Bourget:

"When an American has nothing else to do he can always spend some time trying to trace his ancestry back to his grand-father," said Paul Bourget.

"Yes," said Mark Twain, "and when a Frenchman has nothing better to do, he can always try to find out who his father was."

*The gossip column of an English newspaper printed this paragraph:

"James McNeill Whistler and Oscar Wilde were seen yesterday at Brighton talking, as usual about themselves."

Whistler sent the clipping to Wilde with this line, "I wish reporters would be more accurate. You may remember, Oscar, we were talking about me."

Wilde answered, "True, Jimmie, we were talking about you—but I was thinking about myself."

*In Dublin's Moore Street, the American tourist picked up a melon and jokingly asked the stallholder:

"Say, is this the biggest apple you can grow around here?"

She turned with cool cynicism and calmly told him, "Buy that grape or put it down."

*Bessie Braddock and Winston Churchill:

"Winston, you're drunk."

"Bessie, you're ugly. But tomorrow I shall be sober, and you'll still be ugly."

*A highly placed member of the Convention during the French Revolution attempted to wither an opponent of lower origin by asking:

"Is it true, as I have been told that the member from X is a veterinary?"

The member from X replied:

"Yes, Monsieur. Are you ill?"

*The guest speaker was an hour late, and the college audience was growing restless. The chairman, hoping to salvage the evening, whispered to Professor Getz, famed for his wit, to get up and say a few words.

The professor stepped to the platform and, by way of breaking the ice, remarked, "I've just been asked by the chairman to come up and say something funny."

At which point a student heckler in the back of the hall called out, "You'll tell us when to laugh, won't you?"

Professor Getz, deadpan but quick, said, "Sure, I'll tell. The others will know."

*The girl glanced quickly at the half-pint youth who had just asked her for a dance.

"I'm sorry," she replied haughtily, "but I never dance with a child."

Unsquelched, the young man bowed deeply.

"Oh, I beg your pardon," he said. "I didn't know your condition."

*A young man walks into a liquor store and asks the hard-bitten old clerk for a bottle of gin. The clerk thinks he sees an opportunity to have some fun, and so he asks, "Well, what kind of gin, young fellow? We have three kinds, you know. There is oxygen, hydrogen, and nitrogen."

The customer is not unsophisticated as all that, so he thinks a minute and then answers, "Oh is that so? Very interesting! I didn't know that before. It's strange how things come in threes. Mustard, custard, and you, you bustard."

*Two English boys were bitter enemies. One became an admiral; the other a bishop. Years later, they met on a London railroad platform. The bishop, who had grown fat, swept up to the admiral resplendent in his glittering uniform and said,

"Station master, from which platform does the ten fifteen leave for Oxford?"

The admiral promptly replied,

"Platform five, madam, but in your condition, should you be traveling?"

*When in England, at a fairly large conference, Colin Powell was asked by the Archbishop of Canterbury if our plans for Iraq were just an example of empire building by George Bush.

He answered by saying, "Over the years, the United States has sent many of its fine men and women into great peril to fight for freedom beyond our borders. The only amount of land we have ever asked for in return is enough to bury those that did not return."

It became very quiet in the room.

*Then there was a conference in France where a number of international engineers were taking part, including French and Americans. During a break, one of the French engineers came back into the room saying, "Have you heard the latest dumb stunt Bush had done? He has sent an aircraft carrier to Indonesia to help the Tsunami victims. What does he intend to do, bomb them?"

A Boeing engineer stood up and replied quietly, "Our carriers have three hospitals on board that can treat several hundred people; they are nuclear powered and can supply emergency electrical power to shore facilities; they have three cafeterias with the capacity to feed 3000 people three meals a day, they can produce several thousand gallons of fresh water from sea water each day, and they carry half a dozen helicopters for use in transporting victims and injured to and from their flight deck. We have eleven such ships; how many does France have?"

Once again dead silence.

*A US Navy Admiral attending a naval conference that included admirals from the US, English, Canadian, Australian, and French navies.

At a cocktail reception, he found himself standing with a large group of officers that included personnel from most of those countries. Everyone was chatting away in English as they sipped their drinks. A French admiral suddenly complained, "Whereas Europeans learn many languages, Americans learn only English." He then asked, "Why is it that we always have to speak English in these conferences rather than speaking French?"

Without hesitating, the admiral replied "May be it's because the Brits, Canadians, Aussies, and Americans arranged it so you wouldn't have to speak German."

*It seems a fellow from Chicago was visiting a friend in New York, and they were walking down Fifth Avenue together.

"That building there," said the man from Chicago, pointing to one of the big hotels, "How long did it take to put that up?"

"Oh, about two years," said his New York friend. "And that structure—how long did that take?"

"Also about two years, I suppose."

"Not bad. But in Chicago we could have built it in half the time. And that structure—how long did that take?"

"That? The public library?" said the New Yorker, trying to out-boast the Chicagoan. "Less than four months."

"Four months? We could have done it in two. And this one?" said the visitor, pointing to the hundred stories of the Empire State skyscraper.

"I can't say," replied the New Yorker cautiously. "It wasn't there last night."

*A group of Americans, retired teachers went to France on a tour. Robert Whitting, an elderly gentleman of eighty-three arrived in Paris by plane. At the French customs, he took a few minutes to locate his passport in his carry-on.

"Monsieur," the immigration officer asked sarcastically, "you have been to France before?"

Mr. Whitting admitted he had been to France previously.

"Then you should know enough to have your passport ready."

The American said, "The last time I was here, I didn't have to show it."

"Impossible. Americans always have to show your passports on arrival in France."

The American senior gave the French man a long hard look. Then he quietly explained, "When I came ashore at Omaha Beach on D-Day in 1944 to help liberate this country, I couldn't find any Frenchmen to show."

*A Nazi policeman is swaggering down the street with a large Saint Bernard on a leash.

"That's a fine dog you have there," says a Jewish passerby. "What breed is it?"

"He is a cross between a mongrel and a Jew."

"Aha," says the Jew, "Then the dog is related to both of us."

*At the turn of the century many big-city newspapers competed for the most graphic and lurid stories. One such story by the *Sun* prompted the *New York Post* in an editorial to denounce its sister paper as an exponent of yellow-dog journalism. The next day, the *Sun* replied in its editorial pages, "The *Post* has called the *Sun* a 'yellow dog'. The attitude of the *Sun*, however, will continue to be that of any dog toward any post."

Humor in Repartee

It is a swift witty retort.

*"My people," boasted McCourt, "can trace their ancestors back to the King of Tara."

"I suppose they were in the ark with Noah as well," said his friend with dripping sarcasm.

"Not at all. They had their own boat."

*"Do you mind if I smoke?" Oscar Wilde to Sarah Bernhardt.

"I don't care if you burn," Sarah Bernhardt in reply.

*I was standing next to Bob and I said, "When did I get to be taller than you?"

He said, "Don't know. But it doesn't matter."

"Why not?"

"Because you'll never be smarter."

*Dorothy Parker was seldom caught with her wits down:

Clare Booth Luce (meeting Parker in a doorway), "Age before beauty!"

Dorothy Parker (gliding through the door), "Pearls before swine!"

*Constituent: Vote for you? I'd soon vote for the devil!

John Wilkes: And if your friend is not standing?

*Heckler: Speak up, I can't hear you.

Disraeli: Truth travels slowly, but it will reach even you in time.

*Heckler: Don't you wish you were a man?

Agnes McPhail: Yes, don't you?

*Heckler: Go ahead, Al. Tell 'em all you know. It won't take you long.

Al Smith: If I tell 'em all we both know, it won't take me any longer.

*Heckler: I'm a Democrat!

Theodore Roosevelt: May I ask the gentleman why he is a Democrat?

Heckler: My grandfather was a Democrat. My father was a Democrat, and I am a Democrat.

Theodore Roosevelt: My friend, suppose your father was a jackass, what would you be?

Heckler (instantly): A Republican.

*The reply of Charles Sumner to a minister who asked him impertinently why he did not go into the South with his antislavery speeches was "You are trying to save souls from hell, aren't you? Why don't you go there?"

Humor in Irish Bull

A ludicrous, incongruent, or logically absurd statement generally unrecognized as such by its author—the pleasure of pure nonsense.

*Two eminent intellects were leaning against the bar counter at the Player's Club. One of them above the din of clinking glasses remarked, "When I was born I weighed only two and a half pounds.

The other gazed at him in vague amazement.

"Is that so? Did you live?"

"You ought to see me now."

*"Didn't I see you in Buffalo?

"No, I never was in Buffalo.

"Neither was I. It must have been two other fellows."

*Question: "Is that a brother of yours?"

Answer: "Oh! Yes, yes, yes, yes. Now you remind me of it that was a brother of mine. That's William-Bill we called him. Poor old Bill."

Q: "Why? Is he dead, then?"

A: "Ah! Well, I suppose so. We never could tell. There was a great mystery about it."

Q: "That is sad, very sad. He disappeared, then?"

A: "Well, yes in a sort of general way. We buried him."

Q: "Buried him! Buried him, without knowing whether he was dead or not?"

A: "Oh no! Not that. He was dead enough."

Q: "Well, I confess, I can't understand this. If you buried him, and you knew he was dead . . .

A: "No! No! We only thought he was.

Q: "Oh, I see. He came to life again."

A: "I bet he didn't."

Q: "Well, I never heard anything like this. Somebody was dead. Somebody was buried. Now where was the mystery?"

A: "Ah! That's just it. That's it exactly. You see, we were twins—Defunct and I—and we got mixed up in the bathtub when we were only two weeks old, and one of us drowned. But we didn't know which. Some think it was Bill. Some think it was me."

Q: "Well, that is remarkable. What do you think?"

A: "Goodness knows! I would give the whole world to know. This solemn, this awful tragedy has cast a gloom over my whole life. But I will tell you a secret now, which I have never revealed to any creature before. One of us had a peculiar mark, a large mole on the back of his left hand—that was me. That child was the one that was drowned."

*"Tell me, Denny," said Barney as he put down the last glass and rose uncertainly to his feet, "do you know where I left my coat?"

"Sure, Barney," said the friend. "You got it on."

"Thanks for telling me. And it's a good thing you noticed it, or I'd have gone home without it."

*A professor met a certain friend and said, "Why, I heard that you were dead!"

The fellow replied, "Well, you see that I'm alive."

The professor said, "But I assure you, the man who told me is much more dependable than you."

Humor in Self-Deprecation

The act of belittling oneself, the subject makes himself the object of the joke.

Self-deprecation keeps one in check. It is the healthiest brand of humor, since the only target is you. Self-deprecation humor is the single most important technique one can use to establish instant rapport with the reader or with the audience—provided it is not carried too far to look like self-flagellation. If we accept self-love is the source of evil, then self-deprecation is its antidote provided of course it does not produce an appearance of self-condemnation.

*The classic in self-deprecation: "I would never want to belong to a country club that would have me as a member."(Groucho Marx)

*When Stephen Douglas accused Abraham Lincoln of being two-faced, Lincoln said, "If I had two faces, I certainly wouldn't wear this one."

*At a global warming slide show, the former presidential candidate with power-point clicker in hand, and the first words out of Al Gore's mouth are "Hello, my name is Al Gore, and I used to be the next president of the United States." Students thousands of them roar with laughter, cheers, whistles, applause, and a standing ovation.

*He had the kind of face only a mother could love. If that mother was blind in one eye and had that kind of milky film over the other . . . but still he was my identical twin. (Colin Mochrie, *Whose Line is it anyway?*)

Humor in Limericks

The kind of witty, humorous, or nonsense poem.

The limerick is the only fixed poetic form native to the English language.

It was in the 1880s, when for the first time, the name *limerick* was applied to the present form. It is believed that the name was appropriated from that of the town in Ireland. There used to be a chorus, now forgotten, "Won't you come up to Limerick?"

There are two kinds of limericks.

(a) Limericks that can be told when ladies and children are present and (b) Limericks that cannot be related in the presence of ladies and children. The limericks you will find here can be related in the presence of ladies, children, and even priests and the pope.

A limerick's Admitted a Verse Form

A terse form: A curse form: A hearse form.

It may not be lyric

And at best it's satiric,

And a whale of a tail in perverse form.

The limerick is furtive and mean;

You must keep her in close quarantine,

Or she sneaks to the slums

And promptly becomes

Disorderly, drunk and obscene. (Prof. Morris Bishop)

An Old Archaeologist, Throstle,

Discovered a marvelous fossil.

He knew from its bend

And the knob on its end

'Twas the peter of Paul the Apostle.

There Was a Young Lady of Siam

Who said to her lover Priam,

You can kiss me of course,

But it must be by force,

For God knows you are stronger than I am.

A Cute Curate Who Lived in Dundalk,

Proclaimed he could fly like a hawk,

Cheered by thousands of people,

He leapt from a steeple,

But the splashdown proved it was just plain talk.

The Puritan People of Teeling,

Express all the horror with feeling.

When they see that a chair, has all its legs bare,

They look away straight to the ceiling.

Here lies the body of Sir John Guise.

Nobody laughs, and nobody cries;

Where his soul is and how it fares

Nobody knows and nobody cares.

A diner while dining at Crew

Found quite a large mouse in his stew.

Said the waiter, "Don't shout

And wave it about,

Or the rest will be wanting one too."

To his club-footed child said, Lord Stipple,

As he poured his postprandial tipple:

Your mother's behavior

Gave pain to Our Savior

And that's why He made you a cripple.

There was a young lady called Wylde,

Who kept herself quite undefiled

By thinking of Jesus,

Contagious diseases,

And the bother of having a child.

There was a young girl who begat

Three brats by name Nat, Pat, and Tat.

It was fun in the breeding

But hell in the feeding

When she found there was no tit for Tat.

There was an old man with a beard,

Who said, "It's just as I feared!"

Two owls and a hen,

Four larks and a wren,

Have all built their nests in my beard!"

There was a young lady from Poona

Who sailed along slow like a schooner.

When told that her front

Was enlarged and quite blunt

Said, "Why hasn't the baby come sooner?"

There's a dowager near Sneden Landing

Whose manners are bluff and commanding;

It is one of her jests

To trip up her guests,

For she hates to keep gentlemen standing.

Humor in Personification

It gives human characteristics to inanimate objects, animals, or ideas.

*I am sending you a kiss

That will land on your knee

Climb up your leg

Scramble over your back

And hide in your hair.

Then, when you are to fall asleep

It will bite you gently on your neck

And whisper in your ear, "I love you."

*Hey diddle, diddle,

The cat and the fiddle,

The cow jumped over the moon;

The little dog laughed

To see such sport,

And the dish ran away with the spoon.

*My food loves to prance, to jump, to dance;

I wait for the time, I wait for the chance!

As mommy goes in and out of the room,

Tables and chairs become their ballroom!

I flick my fingers; swing my wrist.

Beans and turkey are doing twist!

Peas, plums, apples or mangos;

On to the walls, they're doing the tango!

*There's a cat named Joe and you wouldn't want to know

But he thinks he'd like to be a hippopotamus

And it sounds very strange, and he really wants to change

And in that way he's just like a lot of us

Oh, it wouldn't be so bad if he was certified as mad

But he's not, he holds a normal conversation

It's just that within he's in a different kind of skin

And it causes him a lot of botheration.

Humor in Tongue Twisters

It is a phrase that is designed to be difficult to articulate properly and can be used as a type of spoken or sung.

Once upon a barren moor

There dwelt a bear, also a boar,

The bear could not bear the boar,

The bear thought the boar was a bore

At last the bear could bear no more.

That boar that bored him on the moor.

And so one morn he bored the boar.

That boar will bore no more.

I'm a pheasant plucker,

I'm a pheasant-plucker's son,

I will be plucking pheasants

'Till the pheasant plucker comes.

*The sixth sick sheik's sixth sheep's sick.

Humor in Epigram

It is a concise, clever, and, often, paradoxical statement or line of verse.

Lord Rochester, an Epigram (epitaph for King Charles II)

Here lies our sovereign lord, King,

Whose promise none relies on;

He never said a foolish thing,

Nor ever did a wise one.

To which the witty monarch rejoined:

"My words are my own, and my actions are my ministers."

On His Books

When I am dead, I hope it may be said:

His sins were scarlet, but his books were read.

(Hilaire Belloc)

On the Politician

Here, richly, with ridiculous display,

The politician's corpse was laid away.

While all of his acquaintance sneered and slanged,

I wept: for I had longed to see him hanged.

Humor in Wordplay

This is a literary technique and a form of wit in which the words that are used become the main subject of the work.

There is a Q to P (K.B.)

Playing with words is a familiar type of humor, and one which children delight in. Much of the pleasure in wordplay is probably the mere delight of exploration, of finding out the possibility in words. There is a delight in merely noticing that a form of words meant to have one meaning can also have an entirely different one. Those who are fascinated by words and wordplay will find this amusing.

*This from Lewis Caroll:

"Take some more tea," the March hare said to Alice very earnestly.

"I've had nothing yet," Alice replied in an offended tone, "so I can't take more."

"You mean you can't take *less*," said the hatter. "It's very easy to take *more* than nothing."

*Whether the weather is cold, or whether the weather is hot, we shall always have weather, whether we want it or not.

*When someone called Will Roger's attention to his ungrammatical use of the word "ain't," he responded, "Maybe ain't, ain't so correct, but I notice that lots of who ain't using ain't, ain't eatin'."

*The class was told, "You have ears to hear, eyes to see, a nose to smell, and feet to run."

"But please, sir," said a child, "my nose runs and my feet smell."

*There is a monastery that's in financial trouble, and in order to increase revenue, it decided to go into the *fish* and *chips* business.

One night a customer raps on the door and a monk answers. The customer says, "Are you the *fish* friar?"

"No," the robed figure replies, "I'm the *chip* monk."

*The dead batteries were given *free of charge.*

*To write with a broken pencil is *pointless.*

*When the smog clears in Los Angeles, *UCLA.*

*A dentist and a manicurist fought *tooth and nail.*

*Bakers trade bread recipes on a *knead*-to-know basis.

*He had a photographic memory which was never *developed.*

Humor in Epitaphs

It is an inscription on a tomb or a grave in memory of one buried there.

*Here lies a father of twenty-nine,

There would have been more

But he didn't have time.

*Dorothy Parker proposed for her gravestone the line: This is on me.

*From a hypochondriac's tombstone: I told you I was sick.

May have added, "And you didn't believe me."

*Epitaph for a waiter: God finally caught his eye.

*Here lies Ann Mann:

She lived an old maid

But died an old Mann.

*On Jonathan Fiddle:

On 22nd of June

Jonathan Fiddle

Went out of tune.

*Mixing it with business:

Sacred to the remains of

Jonathan Thompson

A pious Christian and

Affectionate husband

His disconsolate widow

Continues to carry on

His grocery business

At the old stand as usual.

Main Street; cheapest

And best prices in town.

*On Frank Pixley, editor.

Here *lies* Frank Pixley, as usual.

*In memory of Martha Clay.

Here lies one who lived for others;

Now she has peace. And so have they.

(W. C. Sellar and R. J. Yeatman)

*Epitaph on a party girl.

Lovely Pamela, who found

One sure way to get around

Goes to bed beneath this stone

Early, sober and alone.

(Richard Usborne)

*(Said to have been once found in Bushey Churchyard in Hertfordshire)

Here lies a poor woman who always was tired,

For she lived in a place where help wasn't hired,

Her last words on earth were, "Dear friends, I am going,

Where washing ain't done nor cooking nor sewing,

And everything there is exact to my wishes,

For there they don't eat, there's no washing of dishes,

I'll be where loud anthems will always be ringing

(But having no voice, I'll be out of the singing)

Don't mourn for me now, don't grieve for me never,

For I'm going to do nothing for ever and ever."

*When Samuel Johnson died, he was memorialized by his contemporaries in epitaphs that were less than charitable.

Here lies Sam Johnson—Reader, have a care,

Tread lightly, lest you wake a sleeping bear:

Religious, moral, generous and humane

He was: but self-sufficient, proud, and vain.

Fond of, and overbearing in dispute,

A Christian and a scholar—but a brute.

*Epitaph on the tomb of Shakespeare, said to have been written by the bard himself (spelling modernized):

Good friend, for Jesus sake forbear

To dig the dust enclosed here.

Blest be the man that spares these stones

And cursed be he that moves my bones.

Gallows Humor

It is a type of humor that still manages to be funny in the face of a hopeless situation.

*WC Fields on his deathbed: "I have spent a lot of time searching through the Bible for loopholes.

*The condemned prisoner points to the electric chair and asks the prison warden, "Are you sure this thing is safe?"

*Oscar Wilde was destitute and on his deathbed, "My wallpaper and I are fighting a duel to the death; one or the other of us has to go."

*As Sir Thomas More climbed a rickety scaffold where he would be executed, he said to his executioner, "I pray you, Mr. Lieutenant, see me safely up; and for my coming down, let me shift for myself."

*Draw the curtain, the farce is over. (Rabelais)

*Louisa M. Alcott, writer, said, "Is it not meningitis?"

*Ludwig Van Beethoven, composer, said, "Friends applaud, the comedy is finished."

*Erskine Childers, Irish patriot executed by firing squad, said, "Take a step forward, lads, it will be easier that way."

*A man who is about to be shot by a firing squad, when asked if he would like a last cigarette, refused saying, "No thanks, I'm trying to give up smoking."

Humor in Famous Last Words

*I am bored with it all. (Winston Churchill)

*Turn up the lights, I don't want to go home in the dark. (O. Henry, writer)

*Is everybody happy? I want everybody to be happy. I know I am happy. (Ethel Barrymore, actress)

*That was the best ice-cream soda I ever had. (Lou Costello, comedian)

*Good night, my darlings, I'll see you tomorrow. (Noel Coward, writer)

*That was a great game, fellers. (Bing Crosby)

*I've had a hell of a lot of fun and I've enjoyed every minute of it. (Errol Flynn, actor)

*A king should die standing. (Louis XVIII, king of France)

*I've had eighteen straight whiskies; I think that's a record. (Dylan Thomas, poet)

*I owe much; I have nothing; the rest I leave to the poor.

Draw the curtain, the farce is over. (Francis Rabelais, writer)

*God bless. Goddamn. (James Thurber, humorist)

*Don't let it end like this. Tell them I said something. (Pancho Villa, Mexican revolutionary)

*Curtain! Fast music! Light! Ready for the last finale. Great! The show looks good, the show looks good. (Florenz Ziegfeld, showman)

*All my possessions for a moment. (Queen Elizabeth of England)

*I should never have switched from Scotch to Martini. (Humphrey Bogart)

*How are the receipts at Madison Square Gardens? (P. T. Barnum)

*I am dying. I haven't drunk champagne for a long time. (Anton Pavlovich Chekhov)

*Sir Walter Raleigh, one of nature's true noblemen, was so composed when he went to the scaffold in the Tower of London that he took his pipe with him. He turned to the executioner, ran his thumb over the sharp edge of the axe and remarked, "This is a sharp medicine but it is a physician for all diseases."

Heard by Passengers in Flight

*On landing, the stewardess said, "Please be sure to take all of your belongings. If you're going to leave anything, please make sure it's something we'd like to have."

*From a Southwest Airlines employee:

"Welcome aboard Southwest Flight 245 to Tampa. To operate your seatbelt, insert the metal tab into the buckle, and pull tight. It works like any other seatbelt; and, if you don't know how to operate one, you probably shouldn't be out in public unsupervised."

*In the event of sudden loss of cabin pressure, masks will descend from the ceiling. Stop screaming, grab the mask, and pull it over your face. If you have a small child traveling with you, secure your mask before assisting with theirs. If you are traveling with more than one small child, pick your favorite.

*As you exit the plane, make sure to gather all of your belongings. Anything left behind will be distributed evenly among the flight attendants. Please do not leave children or spouses.

*On a South Western flight (SW has no assigned seating, you just sit where you want), passengers were apparently having a hard time choosing, when a flight attendant announced, "People, people we're not picking out furniture here, find a seat and get in it."

*On a Continental Flight with a very "senior" flight attendant crew, the pilot said, "Ladies and gentlemen, we've reached cruising altitude and will be turning down the cabin lights. This is for your comfort and to enhance the appearance of your flight attendants."

*There may be fifty ways to leave your lover, but there are only four ways out of this airplane.

*Thank you for flying Delta Business Express. We hope you enjoyed giving us the business as much as we enjoyed taking you for a ride.

*Thank you and remember nobody loves you, or your money, more than South West Airlines.

*And from the pilot during his welcome message, "Delta Airlines is pleased to have some of the best flight attendants in the industry. Unfortunately, none of them are on this flight."

*Heard on Southwest Airlines just after a very hard landing in Salt Lake City. The flight attendant came on the intercom and said, "That was quite a bump, and I know what y'all are thinking. I'm here to tell you it wasn't the airline's fault, it wasn't the pilot's fault, it wasn't the flight attendant's fault—it was the asphalt.

Humor in Battle of Wits

This is where the one with a cool head carries the day.

*Annoyed by a man who was cashing a one-cent government check, a bank teller decided to make things difficult for him.

"How old are you?"

"Forty-seven," replied the man.

"What's your wife's name?"

"Mary."

"Any children?"

"Two, a boy of eight and a girl of two."

"Insurance?"

"I have a life policy. The wife and children have endowment policies."

"Belong to any fraternal organizations?"

"Yes. The Odd Fellows."

Seeing the man unperturbed by the questions, the teller grew very sarcastic, "Okay, mister, how will you have it?"

"Heads up" was the reply by the still unperturbed man.

*This about a policeman who was being considered for a promotion to captain.

"Suppose you were involved in a high-speed chase. The car you were chasing sped through the intersection ahead and then all of a sudden, a big battleship moved across the intersection, blocking your way. What would you do?"

The man responded with "Of course, I would sink it."

The interviewers were taken aback and asked, "Just how would you sink it?"

The interviewee quickly replied, "With my submarine!"

Astonished, the interviewers pushed further, "And where did you get the submarine?"

At this point the interviewee pulled out his ace, he said, "The same place you got your battleship."

Humor in Aphorism

It is a concise statement of a principle.

*Two silk worms had a race, they ended in a tie.

*When decorating remember, "Less is more."

*No matter how much you push the envelope, it will still be stationery.

*Time flies like an arrow. Fruit flies like a banana.

*A chicken crossing the road is poultry in motion.

*It wasn't that the man didn't know how to juggle. He just didn't have the balls to do it.

*A wife is like an umbrella. After all, before long one takes a cab.

*If confusion is the first step to knowledge, I must be a genius.

*If I can be of any help, you're in worse trouble than I thought.

*If it weren't for the last minute, nothing would get done.

*We must believe in luck. For how else can we explain the success of those we don't like.

*The only reason I get lost in thought is because it's unfamiliar territory.

*Everybody wants to save the earth; nobody wants to help Mom do the dishes.

*When skunks duel, wind direction is everything.

*Lead me not to temptation. I can find it myself.

*The less you know, the more you think you know, because you don't know you don't know.

Humor in Alliteration

It is the repetition of the beginning sound of words.

*We take the profit and *pay* them with *praise*.

*Do I delight to die or life desire. (Venus and Adonis)

*And murmuring of innumerable bees.

*In the dreadful dead of dark midnight.

*Much malice mingled with a little wit.

*Time drives the flocks from Feld to fold,

*When rivers rage and rocks grow cold.

*Her brows like bended bows do stand.

Humor in Witty Metaphor

A metaphor is a figure of speech in which an implied comparison is made between two unlike things that actually have something in common.

*By the second act, I realized I'd seen livelier plots in a cemetery.

*Telling a teenager the facts of life is like giving a fish a bath.

*Lawyers and woodpeckers have mighty long bills.

*It is impossible to carry the torch of truth through a crowd without singeing some one's beard.

Humor in Mixed Metaphors

Mixed metaphors are a succession of incongruous or ludicrous comparisons.

*I smell a rat, I seem to see it floating in the air, but we shall nip it in the bud.

*We will burn that bridge when we come to it.

*I am burning the midnight oil at both ends.

*I'm robbing Peter to pay Piper.

*It's not exactly rocket surgery.

*You can't pull the sheep over my eyes.

*It's best not to open that can of wax.

*Once you open a can of worms, they always come home to roost.

*They were up a tree without a paddle.

*He's burning the midnight oil at both ends.

*Grasping at the straw that broke the camel's back.

*You have buttered your bread, now lie in it.

*Those two get on like a house on fire.

*You can beat a dead horse to water, but you can't make him drink.

*I can see the carrot at the end of the tunnel.

*He's got too many oars in the fire.

*That guy's a bullhead in a china shop.

*We don't want this project to snowball into a can of worms.

*We were up the creek in a handbag.

*She grabbed the bull by the horns, and ran with it.

*It's as plain as the egg on your face.

*They need to wake up and smell the music.

*He's suffering from a detached rectum.

*I'm sweating like a bullet.

*He's like a duck out of water.

*From now on, I'm watching everything you do with a fine-tuned comb.

Humor in Malapropism

It's the grotesque or inappropriate use of a word.

*Illiterate him, I say, quite from your mind, ordered Mrs. Malaprop.

*As for Mrs. Malaprop's educational theories, she says that she would not wish a daughter of hers to be a *progeny* of learning but would amongst other things have her instructed in geometry, so that "she might know something of the *contagious* countries."

*I was so hungry that I gouged myself.

*She don't like me and I don't like her, so it's neutral.

*Chairman, to his directors, "Gentlemen, last month we were teetering on the edge of a precipice. Today we are going to take a great leap forward."

*Your contemptuous treatment of me is a great humility.

*In small European towns, markets were the hublub of activity.

*The Bible forbids fortification.

*The only activity our grandchildren are interested in at the circus is going on the cannibal rides.

Humor in Doggerel and Ditties

It is a derogatory term for verse; the word very likely derived from dog.

Said the big red rooster

To the little brown hen,

"You haven't laid an egg

Since goodness knows when"

Said the little brown hen

To the big red rooster:

"You don't come along as often as you used to."

Here's good rule of thumb;

Too clever is dumb.

What's the use.

Sure, deck your limbs in pants;

The limbs are yours, my sweeting.

You look divine as you advance

Have you seen yourself retreating?

(Kenneth Bain)

Too late to lament

A certain young lady said, "Pa"

That week you came home from Ba

And got out your ejector

Without its protector—

Now look! Once again I'm Ma.

(Anonymous)

That's a Lovely Dress You're Almost Wearing

The lady wore an evening gown

And when she went about

She'd think that she was inside it,

While much of her was out.

Which, in passing,

I might mention,

Was, of course,

Her clear intention.

(Kenneth Bain)

When pursued by a cloud of bees

You should always seek sanctuaries.

When you've found one

And closed the door,

So the bees aren't with you

Any more,

You can safely say sanctuary

Much

Preferably in Dutch

Which bees don't speak very much.

Not being one of uzz

They just buzz.

(Kenneth Bain)

I wonder why

As time goes by

We cherish less

The things we've got

And yearn the more

For what we've not.

(Anonymous)

Some of the time in my languorous life

Has been spent at the breasts

Of another man's wife.

(Kenneth Bain)

Here lies the body of Rachel Jones

Who died of eating, chicken bones

Her name was Smith

And was not Jones

But Jones was used

To rhyme with bones.

(Anonymous)

Humor in Bumper Stickers

*Single Mormon seeks several spouses.

*I am not a bum, my wife works.

*If you drink like a fish, swim, don't drive.

*Women have to be in the mood; Men just have to be in the room.

*Don't wait for the hearse to take you to church.

*As long as there are tests, there will be prayer in schools.

*A smile is contagious. Let's make it an epidemic.

Humor in Zeugma

Use the same word to describe two things, one thing that goes with it and one that doesn't necessarily fit—a figure of speech in which one verb controls two different objects each in a different sense.

*After two unsuccessful marriages, I find myself keeping my guard up, along with my underpants.

*Whenever I stop at Shop Wright, I get a bottle of perfume and a headache.

*The addict kicked the habit and then the bucket.

*She went straight home in a flood of tears, and a sedan chair. (Charles Dickens)

*You can leave in a taxi. If you can't get a taxi, you can leave in a huff. If that's too soon, you can leave in a minute and a huff. (Groucho Marx from *Duck Soup*)

Humor in Understatement (Meiosis)

It is a form of speech which contains an expression of less length than what would be expected—saying less in order to mean more.

*The all-time favorite is by Mark Twain: "The reports of my death are grossly exaggerated."

*Waiting to be whipped is the most uninteresting period of boyhood life.

*To find oneself locked out of a country house at half-past two in the morning in a pair of lemon-colored pajamas can never be an unmixedly agreeable experience. (P. G. Wodehouse)

*Albert Einstein prefaces a volume on *Special and General Theory of Relativity* with the hope that "This book may bring someone a few hours of suggestive thought."

*Shakespeare in Romeo and Juliet (Act 2, scene 1)

*Mercutio describes his mortal wound, "Not so deep as a well nor so wide as a church door; But 'tis enough, twill serve."

*Few things so speedily modify an uncle's love as a nephew's air gun bullet in the fleshy part of the leg. (P. G. Wodehouse)

*The fascination of shooting as a sport depends almost wholly on whether you are at the right or wrong end of the gun. (P. G. Wodehouse)

Except for the slight bias toward dishonesty which led her to steal everything she could lay her hands on which was not nailed down, Aileen Peavey was an admirable character.

Humor in Exaggeration or Hyperbole

It is an overreach—to represent as greater than is actually the case.

The easiest way to make things laughable and yet get your point across is to exaggerate to the point of absurdity their salient traits.

*Ann Coulter's description of 9/11 widows as self-obsessed witches enjoying their husband's deaths.

*At the National Press Club, Senator Rick Santorum alerted Americans of the Islamists' dream of "a new global caliphate where Islamic fascism will rule mankind."

*Heard in *Fox News*: Is *National Public Radio* an agent of Jihadist Inquisition?

*I wouldn't say the rooms in my last hotel were small, but the *mice were hunchbacked*. (Fred Allen)

*In *Antony and Cleopatra*, Cleopatra praises Antony: His legs bestrid the ocean: his reared arm crested the world.

*An angler tells a listener that he has caught a very large fish. The listener is expectant. "It was so big that"—the listener is on tiptoes—"when I pulled it out the level of the water in the lake sank two feet"—expectation is disillusioned and the listener laughs.

*My mother-in-law is so fat that she uses the refrigerator for her lunch box.

Humor in Irony

A situation if the actions taken have an effect exactly opposite from what was intended.

There are various kinds of irony:

- Verbal irony—where what you mean to say is different from the words you use.
- Situational irony—comprises what is expected to happen with what actually does happen.
- Dramatic irony—uses a narrative to give the audience more information about the story than the character knows.

*In 1981 President Reagan was hit in the chest by a bullet fired by John Hinkley, which ricocheted off the car's bulletproof window. Isn't it ironical that the very technology that was intended to protect (bulletproof window) contributed to his near-fatal injuries?

*Ozymandias of Egypt

Another name was Ramesses the Great, Pharaoh of the nineteenth dynasty of ancient Egypt. The sonnet paraphrases the inscription on the base of the statue, as "King of Kings am I, Ozymandias. *If anyone would know how great I am and where I lie, let him surpass one of my works."*

And this is what becomes of all the grandeur as related by Percy Bysshe Shelley in the poem, "Ozymandias." It is Shelley's effort to make us realize the brevity and emptiness of fame.

I met a traveler from an antique land

Who said: Two vast and trunk-less legs of stone Stand in the desert. Near them, on the sand,

Half sunk, a shattered visage lies, whose frown,

Tell that its sculptor well those passions read

Which yet survive, stamped on these lifeless things,

The hand that mocked them, and the heart that fed;

And on the pedestal these words appear:

"My name is Ozymandias, king of kings:

Look on my works, ye Mighty, and despair!"

Nothing beside remains. Round the decay

Of that colossal wreck, boundless and bare

The lone and level sands stretch far away.

Author O. Henry comes up with classic ironies in his brilliant short stories.

*In "In after "Twenty Years," two friends who had a pact to meet after twenty years find that one of them is a robber and the other is a cop. So in spite of being friends, the cop has to arrest the robber that night.

*In "The Cop and the Anthem," the main character who is a petty thief lies on a bench one lazy day and finally decides that he will turn over a new leaf. Only to find in the next instant to have a cop arrest him for loitering about.

Humor in Lyrics

They are set of words that make up a song, usually consisting of verses and choruses.

To get the most out of lyrics, in most cases, they must be accompanied by music. "The wit of the witty lyric," it is said, "evaporates as soon as it comes out of the end of the transcriber's pen."

Some people say a man is made outta mud

A poor man's made outta muscle and blood

Muscle and blood and skin and bones

A mind that's weak and a back that's strong.

You load sixteen tons, what do you get

Another day older and deeper in debt.

Saint Peter don't call me 'cause I can't go

I owe my soul to the company store.

I was born one mornin' when the sun didn't shine

I picked up my shovel and I walked to the mine

I loaded sixteen tons of number nine coal

And the straw boss said, "well, a-bless my soul"

You load sixteen tons, and what do you get

Another day older and deeper in debt

Saint Peter don't you call me 'cause I can't go

I owe my soul to the company store.

I was born one mornin' it was drizzlin' rain

Fightin' and trouble are my middle name

I was raised in the canebrake by my an ol' mama lion

Cain't no-a-high-toned woman make me walk the line.

You load sixteen tons and what do you get

Another day older and deeper in debt

Saint Peter don't you call me 'cause I can't go

I owe my soul to the company store.

If you see me comin', better step aside

A lotta men didn't, a lotta men died

One fist of iron, the other of steel

If the right one don't a-get you

Then the left one will.

You load sixteen tons, what do you get

Another day older and deeper in debt

Saint Peter don't you call me 'cause I can't go

I owe my soul to the company store.

(Country singer Merle Travis made popular by Tennessee Ernie Ford)

Dropkick me Jesus through the goal posts of life

End over end neither left nor right

Straight through the heart of them righteous uprights

Dropkick me Jesus through the goal posts of life.

Make me, oh make me, Lord more than I am

Make me a piece of your master game plan

Free from the earthly temptation below

I've got the will, Lord, if you've got the toe.

Dropkick me Jesus through the goal posts of life

End over end neither left nor right.

Straight through the heart of them righteous uprights

Dropkick me Jesus through the goal posts of life.

Take all the brothers who've gone on before

And all of the sisters who've knocked on your door

All the departed dear loved ones of mine

Stick 'em up front in the offensive line.

Dropkick me Jesus through the goal posts of life

End over end neither left nor right

Straight through the heart of them righteous uprights

Dropkick me Jesus through the goal posts of life.

Yeah, Dropkick me Jesus through the goal posts of life

End over end neither left nor to right

Straight through the heart of them righteous uprights

Dropkick me Jesus through the goal posts of life.

(Paul Craft)

Sweet Rosie O'Grady

She was a blacksmith by birth.

Rosie got tired of living

And decided to leave this earth.

She swallowed a ruler,

But dying by inches was hard.

So Rosie went down to the alley

And lay down and died by the yard.

(Stevie)

Me and Sue we're making music like never before

When we heard the killing sound of a key in the door

She looked at me, I looked at her.

She said could be my husband I'm not really sure.

Well, out of the bed I scrambled into the boots

Jumped out the window in my birthday suit.

I never dreamed I could move so fast

One step ahead of a shotgun blast.

It was close encounter of the crazy kind

I prayed the Lord don't let the full moon shine

Tonight I'll be grateful if you save my life

Good thing I have an understanding wife.

When I got home the house was totally dark

'Til old Napoleon began to bark.

The lights went on and the door flew open

She stood there staring, I stood there hopin'

She said she's heard a hundred stories from me

There wasn't one that she had ever believed.

I said but this time honey it's the honest truth

I'm standing here as living proof.

I want to be your dominated love slave

I want to be the one that takes the pain

You can spank me when I do not behave

Mack me in the forehead with a chain.

'Cause I love feelin' dirty

And I love feelin' cheap

And I love it when you hurt me

So drive them staples deep.

I want you to slap me and call me naughty

Put a belt sander against my skin

I want to feel pain all over my body

Can't wait to be punished for my sins.

'Cause I love feelin' dirty

And I love feelin' cheap

And I love it when you hurt me

So drive them staples deep.

Yee-hah!

'Cause I love feelin' dirty

And I love feelin' cheap

And I love it when you hurt me

So *drrrriiiveeee* . . . Staples?

Tweedledum and Tweedledee

Agreed to have a battle;

For Tweedledum said Tweedledee

Had spoiled his nice new rattle.

Just then flew down a monstrous crow,

As black as a tar-barrel;

Which frightened both the heroes so,

They quite forgot their quarrel.

Humor in Euphemism

It is the substitution of an inoffensive term for one considered offensively explicit.

We would rather not say she or he died. Instead we go to comical lengths to soften the blow.

*Called home.

*Cashed his checks.

*Kicked the bucket.

*Called beyond.

*Checked out (like a hotel).

*Stepped off the deep end.

*Heard the final call

*Exited

*Bit the dust.

*His number was up.

*Shuffled off.

*Pushing daisies.

*Expired (like magazine subscription)

*Croaked.

*Met his end.

*Crossed over (like on Fifth Avenue)

Gone West.

Gone to his reward.

Departed.

The prize goes to this. One clergyman pointing to the dead man said, "This is only the shell—the nut is gone."

Humor in Double Entendre

It is when a word is used in one sense and then its meaning is switched for comic effect.

*Include your children when baking cookies.

*Police begin campaign to run down jaywalkers.

*Iraqi head seeks arms.

*A female anchor to news anchor who, the day after it supposed to have snowed and didn't, turned to the weatherman and asked, "So, Bob, where's that eight inches you promised me last night?"

*According to one view, the husband is supposed to have *earned a lot* and so put *a bit on the side,* and according to another, the wife is supposed to have been *a bit on the side* and so to have *earned a lot.*

*Mountains and alcohol: the higher you are, the higher you get.

*I hate alcohol. I can't stand drinking—I keep falling down.

*I shot an elephant in my pajamas. How he got in my pajamas I'll never know. (Groucho Marx)

*Panda mating fails; veterinarian takes over.

*Clinton wins budget. More lies ahead.

*Miners refuse to work after death.

*Man struck by lightning faces battery charge.

*Astronaut takes blame for gas in space.

*Kids make nutritious snacks.

*Local high school dropouts cut in half.

*One bachelor asked another, "How did you like your stay at the nudist camp?"

"Well," he answered, "It was OK after a while. The first three days were the hardest."

*One prostitute asked to another, "Can you lend me ten dollars until I get back on my back?"

Humor in Funny Imagery

*Her face has more lifts than the Empire State Building.

*A full mouth big enough to seat a family of six.

*A laughter that sounds like someone smashing up several industrial-sized conservatories.

*A yodelly yawn.

*Don't be an old stick in the mud: old fashioned.

*I feel as though I was using a sword against cobwebs.

*I have to keep my mouth shut and burn holes in the lining of my stomach.

*It isn't merely the mother of all hangovers she has. It's the mother-in-law.

*My brain went into screensaver mode.

Humor in Funny Similes

It is when you compare two things using the word like *and* as.

*My mouth's as dry as Gandhi's flip-flop.

*I am off like a bride's nightie.

*Don't just stand there like a bump on a log.

*Teeth like a burnt-out fuse box.

*Sweating like Pavarotti on a treadmill.

*As welcome as a skunk at a lawn party.

*Act like a shepherd and get the flock out of here.

*You've taken as many positions on this matter as in Karma Sutra.

*As slow as the second coming of Christ.

*As welcome as a fart in a crowded elevator.

*Happy as a dog with two tails.

*As annoying as a scratch you cannot reach.

*He was like a cock who thought that the sun had risen to hear him crow.

*John and Mary never met. They were like two humming birds who had also never met.

*We were odorless like Adam and Eve before the Fall.

*Except during actual meals, dishes had to be invisible as underwear.

*As an inescapable part of being young and female like menstruation.

*The escapades have a ring of the Keystone cops colliding with Marx Brothers.

Humor in Onomatopoeia (Echoism)

It is using words that sound like their meaning—where the appeal is to the ear of the reader rather than the eye—as in the hiss of the goose, the click of the camera, and the morning cry of cock-a-doodle-doo.

I'm getting married in the morning.

Ding Dong the bells are gonna chime.

(Lerner and Loewe in *My Fair Lady*)

Mom and Dad are home.

Slam! Slam!

Go the car doors.

Jangle! Jangle!

Go the house keys.

Jiggle! Jiggle!

Go the keys in the door.

Squeak!

Goes the front door!

Thump! Thump!

That is me running down the stairs.

Guess what? Mom and Dad are home!

The Game.

Clap! Clap!

Stomp! Stomp!

Swish! Swish!

This is the way we get through.

Our games.

The crowd shouts,

"Yahoo!"

The ball soars through the air.

Then, bounce, bounce, bounce.

The audience holds its breath.

Swish!

The ball goes in;

We win.

Camping.

Crack! Crack!

The fire crackles under the stars.

Sizzle! Sizzle!

The water sizzles above the fire.

Crunch! Crunch!

The campers crunching on potato chips.

Click! Clack! Click! Clack!

The tent poles clicking and clacking together.

Rustle! Rustle!

As we prepare our sleeping bags to go to sleep.

Chirp! Chirp!

The crickets say, "good-night."

To Grandma's we go.

Rumble! Rumble!

The thunder roars.

Drip! Drip!

The rain comes down.

Boom! Boom!

The thunder shakes the windowpanes.

Run to the car! Run to the car!

Splash! Splash!

To Grandma's we go,

For hot cocoa.

Zoom! Zoom!

Pool party.

Squeal!

Kids are running everywhere.

Running and splashing,

Falling in the pool.

The music plays.

Stomp! Stomp!

The children dance.

Finally, the food is off the grill.

Munch, munch, munch!

(Natasha Niemi)

Humor in Ads

*Alka-Seltzer:

Plop, Plop, Fizz, Fizz,

What a relief it is.

*Rice Krispies make a "snap," "crackle," "pop"

When one pours on milk.

*Road Safety:

Clunk, click every trip.

Click the seat belt on after

Clunking the door closed

Click, clack, front and back

Click it or ticket.

*Pancake:

Rooty, tooty, fresh, 'n fruity.

*Post Office:

If it fits; it ships.

Humor in Chiasmus

It is a poetic figure in which two words appear twice in the following order: ABBA.

*Middle age is when

Work is a lot less fun

And fun a lot more work.

*Whenever I stop to shop,

I generally shop until I stop.

*A babysitter is a teenager acting like an adult while the adults are out acting like teenagers.

*When I came to this country, I hadn't a nickel in my pocket, now I have a nickel in my pocket. (Groucho Marx)

*I live not in order to eat, but eat in order to live.

*If you fail to prepare; you must be prepared to fail.

Humor in Tautology

It is saying the same thing twice.

*The plumber fixed our *hot water heater.*

*I made it with *my own hands* for you.

*This is indeed a *sad misfortune.*

*Say it over *again once more.*

Bits and *pieces. First and foremost*

*The group wanted to climb to the very *summit at the top* of the mountain.

Suspense thriller.

*The wall was marred by a *small, tiny speck* of paint.

*A *huge great, big* man.

*The vote was *completely* and *totally* unanimous.

*A *puzzling problem,* isn't it?

An extract from George Carlin's *When Will Jesus Bring the Pork Chops.*

> My fellow countrymen, I speak to you as *coequals,* knowing you are deserving of the *honest truth.* And let me *warn* you *in advance,* my *subject matter* concerns *serious crisis* caused by an event in my *past history:* the *execution-style killing* of a security guard of a delivery truck. At that *particular point in time,* I found myself in *deep depression,* making *mental errors* which seemed as though they might threaten my *future plans.* I am not *over-exaggerating.*

I need a *new beginning,* so I decided to do a *social visit* to a *personal friend* with whom I share the *same mutual* objectives and who is *one of the most unique* individuals I have ever *personally* met.

Humor in Assonance

It is called internal rhyming.

*I measure and treasure the pleasure.

*Yonder there I ponder where to wander.

*New born words like birds that thirst.

*Slow the flow of its inner glow.

*Eyes to my surprise which otherwise.

*A butter flutter and a tiny litter.

*Dancing, prancing free of glancing.

*Find my mind in a place so kind.

*Of certain hues I choose to use.

Humor in Riddles

The old and the young welcome the challenge of a riddle.

There is in the breast of every one of us a little child. That child-like wonder never leaves us. Friends! It's never too late to discover the kid inside us.

The inability to answer a riddle can also be a humbling, teaching experience as it was with Homer. A little beggar boy once asked Homer, "If you catch it you kill it, if not you take it with you. What is it?" Homer thought about it for weeks and could not find the answer. The boy finally gave the answer—lice. It is said Homer felt so humiliated, he killed himself.

*What did the big firecracker say to the little firecracker?

My pop's bigger than your pop.

*What time of day was Adam created?

A little before Eve.

*When a man marries, how many wives does he get?

Sixteen: Four richer, four poorer, four better, four worse.

*A cowboy rides on Friday, stays three consecutive days, and leaves on Friday. How does he do it?

His horse's name is Friday.

*What is the best advice you can give to a worm?

"Sleep late."

*How is business?

Tailor: Oh, it's so-so.

Electrician: It's fairly light.

Author: All right.

Farmer: It's growing.

Astronomer: Looking up.

Elevator operator: Well, it has its ups and downs.

Trash collector: It's picking up.

*What training do you need to be a garbage collector?

None: You just pick it up as you go along.

*Why didn't Noah fish very often?

He had only two worms.

*Which two words have the most letters in them?

Post Office.

*What did the big hand on the clock say to the little hand?

"I'll be around in an hour."

*What is the first sign that a computer is getting old?

It has memory problems.

*How many items can you put in an empty grocery bag?

One. After that, the bag isn't empty any more.

*What did the baby corn say to the mama corn?

Where's popcorn?

*What did one eye say to the other eye?

Something's come between us that smells.

*How is a crossword puzzle like an argument?

One word leads to another.

*Why doesn't a bike stand up by itself?

Because it's two-tired.

*Teacher: Which month has twenty-eight days in it?

Johnny thought for a moment and replied: they all have.

*Why did the farmer name his hog, ink?

Because he kept running out of the pen.

*Why does a cow wear a bell?

Their horns don't work.

Humor in Bad Grammar, Slips, Stumbles, and Verbal Blunders

Artemus Ward coined the word "ingrammaticisms."

*There is probably more promersing and virtuous young men in Toledo than there is anywhere.

*Some have difficulty with socks and shoes. It comes out "shocks and soos."

*When a feller once gets it into his head that *female women* are all after him, you might just as well dispute with the wind as argue with him.

*His wife's mother on the female side.

*Nip it in the butt for nip it in the bud.

*What if worse comes to worse for worst comes to worst.

Humor in bon mot

Bon mot is a clever remark or quick with the quip.

*When someone suggested that Thomas Edwards was just as good as William Warburton, Samuel Johnson shut him up: "A fly, sir, may sting a stately horse and make him wince; but one is but an insect, and the other is a horse still."

*Yes, we must indeed all hang together or assuredly we shall all hang separately. (Benjamin Franklin)

*You hesitate to stab me with a word, and know not silence is the sharper sword. (Samuel Johnson)

*Let me smile with the wise and feed with the rich. (Samuel Johnson)

Humor in Jolly Tall Tales

From American Tall Tales by Mary Pope Osborne. It's a story with unbelievable elements related as if it were true and factual.

Tall tales are entertaining to children and adults alike. They are actual people but their feats of courage and endurance were greatly exaggerated so much so they have now become folk heroes. Americans love to tell these tall tales around campfires and cracker barrels, and with each telling the tales get bigger, better, and boastful. This certainly is an integral part of the American heritage.

There are many legendary heroes. Mike Fink, Wild Bill Hickok, Billy the Kid, Jesse James, Buffalo Bill, and so on. I give below some samples.

Davy Crockett walked like an ox, ran like a fox, and swam like an eel. He liked to tell folks, "When I was a baby, my cradle was the shell of a six hundred pound turtle. I ate so much bear meat and drank so much buffalo milk I could whip my weight in wild cats."

Mose was eight feet tall and hands as large as Virginia hams. "His arms were so long that he could scratch his knee caps without bending his back. He could cross the Hudson River with two breast strokes and with six he could swim all the way around the Island of Manhattan."

Pecos Bill: "the greatest cowpuncher ever known on either side of the Rockies, from Texas through Montana and on to Canada. When he was a little baby he was as tough as a pine knot. He teethed on horse shoes instead of teddy bears. He invented roping. Some say his rope was exactly as long as the equator; others argue it was two feet shorter."

John Henry: "When John Henry was born the sky was as black as coal, thunder rolled through the heavens, and earth trembled. His arms were as thick as stovepipes. He had great broad shoulders and strong muscles. And as folks stared at him, he opened his eyes and smiled a smile that lit up the southern night."

Paul Bunyan: One year when it rained from St. Patrick's Day till the Fourth of July, Paul Bunyan got disgusted because his celebration of the Fourth was spoiled. He felt he had to do something about it. He was not the kind who is wont to say this is my karma and let it pass. He dived into Lake Superior and swam to where a solid pillar of water was gushing down. He dived under this pillar, swam up into it, and climbed with powerful swimming strokes and was gone about an hour. He then came splashing down, and as the rain stopped, he explained, "I turned the damn thing off."

Humor in Oxymoron

A figure of speech that combines contradicting terms.

*Old news.

*Thank god, I'm an atheist.

*Accurate estimate.

*Turned up missing.

*Act naturally.

*Smaller half.

*Anxious patient.

*Reagan memoirs.

*Thinking out loud.

*Removable sticker.

*Tight slacks.

*Single copy.

*Numbing sensation.

*Unsolved mystery.

*Doing nothing.

*Original copy.

Humor in Parody

A work created to mock, comment on, or make fun at an original work, a comic imitation of a serious poem.

Parody on Hamlet's "To be or not to be."

I ask to be, or not to be

That is the question, I ask of me.

This sullied life, it makes me shudder.

My uncle's boffing dear, sweet mother.

Would I, could I take my life?

Could I, should I end this strife?

Should I jump out of a plane?

Or throw myself before a train?

Should I from a cliff just leap?

Could I put myself to sleep?

Shoot myself, or take some poison?

May be try self-immolation?

To shuffle off this mortal coil,

I could stab myself with a fencing foil.

Slash my wrists while in the bath?

Would it end my angst and wrath?

To sleep, to dream, now there's the rub.

I could drop a toaster in the tub.

Would all be glad, if I were dead?

Could I perhaps kill them instead?

This line of thought takes consideration—

For I'm the king of procrastination.

(From *Green Eggs and Hamlet*)

'Twas the night before Christmas. For bikers unknown.

'Twas the night before Christmas, and all through the Pad,

There was nada happenin', now that's pretty bad.

The woodstove was hung up in that stocking routine,

In hopes that the *Fat Boy* would soon make the scene.

With our stomachs packed with Tacos and Beer,

My girl and I crashed on the couch for some cheer.

When out in the yard there arose such a racket,

I ran for the door and pulled on my jacket.

I saw a large bro on a '56 *Pan,*

Wearin' black leathers, a cap, and boots (cool biker, man)

He hauled up the bars on that bikeful of sacks,

And that Pan hit the roof like it was running on tracks.

I couldn't help gawking, the old guy had class.

But I had to go in—I was freezing my ass.

Down through the stovepipe he fell with a crash,

And out of the stove he came dragging his stash.

With a smile and some glee he passed out the loot,

A new jacket for her and some parts for my scoot.

He patted her fanny and shook my right hand,

Spun on his heel and up on the roof came a great deal of thunder,

As that massive V-Twin ripped the silence asunder.

With eard in the wind, he roared off in the night,

Shouting, "Have a cool Yule, and to all a good ride."

Anonymous.

Father William Parodies

*"You are old, Father William," the young man said,

And your hair now should be very white;

But it's black and it's bushy all over your head;

Do you think, at your age, this is right?"

"It's touched up," Father William replied to his son,

"And with transplants my baldness is ended;

Though I'm now eighty-four, I appear forty-one,

And the chicks think I'm groovy and splendid."

"You are old," said the youth, "and I thought I would find

That your face would be sagging and wrinkling;

But your skin is as smooth as a baby's behind

And of lines there is scarcely an inkling."

"Had a face-lift," the old man replied, "just last year;

Cost a bundle, but now I feel human;

I used to come on like Redd Fox or Will Geer,

But now I'm hot stuff like Paul Newman."

"You are old," said the youth, "for despite your new look,

You are bogged down in hopeless senility;

With chicks you come off as a helpless old schnook,

Despite all your claims of virility."

"Shut your face," Father William replied, "though it's true

That I purchased new glands last September,

Whatever I'd hoped for my body to do,

My mind is too old to remember."

(Frank Jacobs)

*"You are old, Father William," the young man cried;

"The few locks which are left you are grey;

You are hale, Father William, a hearty old man:

Now tell me the reason, I pray."

"In the days of my youth," Father William replied,

"I remembered that youth would fly fast,

And abused not my health and my vigor at first,

That I never might need them at last . . ."

(Robert Southey)

*"You are old, Father William," the young man said,

"And your hair has become very white;

And yet you incessantly stand on your head

Do you think, at your age, it is right?"

"In my youth," Father William replied to his son,

"I feared it might injure the brain;

But now that I'm perfectly sure I have none,

Why, I do it again and again . . ."

(Lewis Carroll)

Against Idleness and Mischief

How doth the little busy bee

Improve each shining hour,

And gather honey all the day

From every opening flower!

In works of labor or of skill,

I would be busy too;

For Satan finds some mischief still

For idle hands to do.

(Dr. Isaac Watts)

*How doth the little crocodile

Improve his shining tail,

And pour the waters of the Nile

On every golden scale!

How cheerfully he seems to grin,

How neatly spreads his claws,

And welcomes little fishes in

With gently smiling jaws!

(Lewis Carroll's rendition)

The Star

*Twinkle, twinkle, little star

How I wonder what you are!

Up above the world so high,

Like a diamond in the sky.

(Jane Taylor)

*Twinkle, twinkle, little bat!

How I wonder what you're at!

Up above the world you fly,

Like a tea-tray in the sky.

(Lewis Carroll's rendition)

*Twinkle, Twinkle little star

How I wonder what you are?

Up above the world so high

Like a diamond in the sky

Well I'll tell you little star

I can't tell you what you are

With the smoke and haze and pall

I'm not sure you're there at all.

The Passionate Shepherd to his Love

Come live with me and be my love,

As man and wife, 'neath God above;

We're sure to find eternal bliss—
With open marriage we can't miss.

No joys will equal yours and mine,
Partaking of a love divine,
And should we find that life's a bore,
We'll swing with Jane and Bob next door.
Or, maybe, if it's opportune,
We'll move into a sex commune
And mix it up with studs and chicks
In orgies watching porno flicks.
Perhaps you'll dig companionship
With leather gear and boots and whip;
If so, my love, I'll serve you well
And let you chain me in a cell.
So wed me now, my precious thing,
And be my wife and wear my ring;
Yes, let our married days begin
So we won't have to live in sin.

If

If you can buck a mob of lady shoppers
And get outside without a scratch or bite;
If you can get a dentist for your choppers
To fix a toothache on a Sunday night;

If you can smack a truck with your jalopy

And make the driver think he was to blame;

If you can be a loafer, poor and sloppy,

Yet have the world think you're some famous name;

If you can change a tire on the thruway,

While stranded in the busy center lane;

If you can find a foolproof, tried—and—true way

To housebreak an impossible Great Dane;

If you can find another way to open

A sardine tin when you have lost the key;

If you can find a fumbled bar of soap in

Your shower when the suds won't let you see;

If you can rid your house of dull relations

By faking mumps or plague or Asian flu;

If you can go through tax investigations

And somehow wind up with them owing you;

If you can read these verses as we list 'em

And answer "Yes" to each and every one;

Then, Charlie, you have really licked the system—

And now we wish you'd tell us how it's done.

Sing a Song of Spillage

Sing a song of spillage—

A tanker's fouled the shore;

Four-and-twenty black birds—

They were white before.

Four Little Tigers

Four little tigers

Sitting in a tree;

One became a lady's coat—

Now there's only three.

Three little tigers

'Neath a sky of blue;

One became a rich man's rug—

Now there's only two.

Two little tigers

Sleeping in the sun;

One a hunter's trophy made

Now there's only one.

One little tiger

Waiting to be had;

Oops! He got the hunter first—

Aren't you kind of glad?

Little Bo Peep

Little Bo Peep

Has lost her sheep

And thinks they may be roaming;

They haven't fled;

They've all dropped dead

From nerve gas in Wyoming.

Extracts from Night before Christmas

"You'll note I've arrived with no reindeer this year,

And without them, my sleigh is much harder to steer;

Although I would like to continue to use them,

The wildlife officials believe I abuse them.

To add to my problem, Ralph Nader dropped by

And told me my sleigh was unsafe in the sky;

I now must wear seatbelts, despite my objections,

And bring in the sleigh twice a year for inspections.

Last April my workers came forth with demands,

And I soon had a general strike on my hands;

I couldn't afford to pay unionized elves,

So the missus and I did the work by ourselves.

And if you should ask why I'm glowing tonight,

It's from flying too close to a nuclear site.

He rose from his chair and heaved a great sigh,

And I couldn't help notice a tear in his eye;

"I've tried," he declared, "to reverse each defeat

But I fear that today I've become obsolete."

He slumped out the door and returned to his sleigh,

And these last words he spoke as he went on his way;

"No longer can I do the job that's required";

If anyone asks, just say, "Santa's retired."

Extracts from St. Nicholas Meets the Population Explosion

He panted and sighed like a man who was weary;

His shoulders were stooped and his outlook was dreary:

"I'm way behind schedule," he said with a sigh,

And I've been on the road since the first of July."

'Twas then that I noticed the great, monstrous sack,

Which he barely could hold on his poor, creaking back;

"Confound it!" he moaned, "Though my bag's full of toys,

I'm engulfed by the birthrate of new girls and boys."

Then filling the stockings, he shook his sad face,

"This job is a killer; I can't take the pace;

This cluttered old world is beyond my control;

There even are millions up at the North Pole.

Now I'm late!" he exclaimed, "and I really must hurry!

By now I should be over Joplin, Missouri!"

But he managed to sigh as he drove out of sight,

"Happy Christmas to all, and to all a goodnight!"

Extracts from "The Reagan"

Once he was inaugurated, Reaganomics he created,

Promising a balanced budget, like we had in days of yore;

"Though," he said, "our debt is growing, and a bundle we are owing,

I'll cut taxes, 'cause I'm knowing this will save us bucks galore";

"Please explain," a newsman asked, "how this will save us bucks galore?"

Quoth The Reagan, "Less is more."

During times he wasn't dozing, many plans he was proposing,

Dealing with the deficit, which he no longer could ignore;

"Cuts," he said, "I'm recommending, pending our ascending spending,

With attending trends suspending, then extending as before."

"Does this mean," a newsman asked, "a balanced budget like before?"

Quoth The Reagan, "Nevermore."

Extracts from "In Japan. Sing a Song of Sonys"

Sing a song of Sonys—

A pocketful of yen;

RCA and Zenith

Undersold again;

See the US suffer

From the job we do;

This is how we get revenge

For losing World War II.

In Russia . . . The Old Woman in the Shoe

There was an old woman who lived in a shoe

With Boris, ten kids and a pet kangaroo;

She said, "Though it's cramped and from feet it is smelling,

In Moscow, it's known as a luxury dwelling."

Extract from "Saga of AT&T"

Now we're told all the time, it's a terrible crime

When some giant monopoly rules;

"Competition's the way," the economists say,

Which is what we are taught in our schools;

But from seeing the mess screwing up the US,

Any imbecile plainly can see

Life was better back then in those ancient days when

We were screwed just by AT&T.

Humor in "Comma" Sense

Punctuation is a means, and its end is: helping the reader to hear, to follow.

Misplaced commas have resulted in curious misunderstandings. It is said that an ancient Greek, consulting the oracle at Delphi as to whether he should go to war, was told:

Thou shalt go. Thou shalt return. Never by war shalt thou perish. The Greeks up arms and promptly slain.

Should have been read as:

Thou shalt go thou shalt return never, by war shalt thou perish.

*A woman, without her man, is nothing. and

A woman, without her, man is nothing.

*Every lady in this land

Hath twenty nails on each hand;

Five and twenty on hands and feet;

And this is true, without deceit. and

Every lady in this land has twenty nails.

On each hand, five; and twenty on hands and feet.

And this is true, without deceit.

Huge doctrinal differences hang on the placing of this "innocent" comma as, for instance, in the following illustrations.

*"Verily, I say unto thee, this day thou shalt be with me in Paradise." and

"Verily I say unto thee this day, Thou shalt be with me in Paradise."

*The voice of him that crieth in the wilderness:

Prepare ye the way of the Lord." and

"The voice of him that crieth: In the wilderness prepare ye the way of the Lord."

*"Comfort ye, my people" meaning, go out and comfort my people. and

"Comfort ye, my people" meaning, just cheer up, you lot; it might never happen.

Humor in Satire:

Satire described as the "blessed art" is a literary genre or form by which vices, follies, abuses, and shortcomings are held up to ridicule, ideally with the intent of shaming individuals and society itself into improvement. It's serious writing in a humorous vein. It's considered literature's most exciting and challenging form.

Classic examples of satire are Orwell's *Animal Farm*, Cervantes *Dialogue of the Dogs* and Heller's *Catch 22*.

Henry Carey wrote this poem ("Namby Pamby") as a satire of Ambrose Philips and published it in his *Poems on Several Occasions.*

Philips was a figure who had become politically active and was a darling of the Whig Party. The poem begins with a mock-epic opening calling all the muses to witness the glory of Philips.

"All ye Poets of the Age!

All ye Witlings of the Stage!

Learn your Jingles to reform!

Crop your Numbers and Conform:

Let your little Verses flow

Gently, Sweetly, Row by Row:

Let the Verse the subject fit;

Little Subject, Little Wit.

Namby Pamby is your Guide;

Albion's Joy, Hibernia's Pride."

Great Idea Didn't Work

God so loved the world

That he gave his only forgotten son

To save the world

Into which he was hurled

As a carpenter, no less,

From Nazareth.

Saving what and who?

Now I've forgotten too.

Have you?

Anyway whatever it was

It didn't add up to much because

Two thousand years on the world's a mess

Full of anger and distress.

Do I digress?

No. But I could be at risk

Of becoming an atheisk.

(Kenneth Bain)

Humor in Acrostic Poems

It is one that uses a word or phrase usually the theme or the underlying subject matter of the poem written vertically

For Cat Lovers

Cute and cuddly

Always up to mischief

Time is always spent playing

Stupendous fun.

For Dog Lovers

Dashing, daring, delightful

Oh he's under the table

Growling is a bad thing

Shh go to bed.

For Actors and Actresses

Does anyone realize all the

Ridiculous things

Actors and actresses

Must endure before hearing the

Applause.

Humor in Pun

It is two strings of thought with an acoustic knot.

Pun has got a bad rap. It is also called gramatical humor and, dry cerebral sport; Aristotle called it "educated insolence"; and Samuel Johnson, "false wit."

*There was a man who entered a local paper's *pun* contest. He sent in ten different puns, in the hope that at least one of the puns would win. But unfortunately *no pun in ten did.*

*In England they do not have a *kidney bank*, but they have a *Liverpool.*

*It is better to have loved a short person and lost

Than never to have loved a *tall.*

*A diplomat is one who *lies* abroad for the benefit of his country.

*Interviewer: "Do you consider *clubs* appropriate for small children?"

W. C. Fields: "Only when kindness fails."

*Colds can be positive or negative. Sometimes the *ayes* have it, sometimes the *noes.*

*An Oxford scholar, meeting a porter who was carrying a hare through the streets, accosted him with this extraordinary question—"Prithee, sir, is that thy own *hare* or a wig?"

*A well-born and over-life size lady—every *yard* a queen.

*The weather tonight is like Queen Victoria "long to *reign* over us."

*He often broke into a song he couldn't find the *key.*

*Every calendar's days are *numbered.*

*A boiled egg in the morning is *hard to beat.*

*A man walks into a psychiatrist's office wearing only shorts made of plastic wrap. The shrink says, "Well, I can clearly see you're nuts."

*I bet the butcher the other day that he couldn't reach the meat that was on the top shelf. He refused to take the bet, saying the *steaks were too high.*

Humor in Ambiguity

*A cannibal returning home one evening, asking if he is late for dinner, and is told:

"Yes, everybody's eaten."

*An idiot driving to Chicago. He comes to a sign, "Chicago Left"; Swears to himself, then turns around and heads back home.

*Someone asks a farmer how *long* cows should be milked, and the farmer replies, "The same as *short* ones of course."

Humor in Comical Figures of Speech

*Lance said, "It's horrible to hear lies from her mouth like bees from a hive hot in the sun." (Robin Jeffers)

*Often a hen who has only laid an egg will cackle as though she had laid an asteroid. (Mark Twain)

*He gave her a look that you could have poured on a waffle. (Lardner)

*He generally slept with his mouth open that you could read his inmost thoughts. (Nye)

Humor in Palindrome

It is a word or sentence that reads the same forward as it does backward.

John Taylor wrote the first palindrome recorded in the English language.

In Sentences

*As I pee sir I see Pisa.

*Ma is a nun as I am.

*Madam I am Adam.

*Able was I ere I saw Elba.

*Draw, O coward.

*Ma is as selfless as I am.

*Rise to vote sir.

*Step on no pets.

*So many dynamos.

In Words

*Civic

*Deified

*Radar

*Rotor

*Refer

Humor in Boners

A boner is a howler, a misprint, or a right word in the wrong place.

*Abraham Lincoln wrote the Gettysburg Address while *traveling* from Washington to Gettysburg *on the back of an envelope.*

*Columbus was a navigator who *cursed* about the Atlantic.

*They gave William IV a lovely funeral. It took *six men to carry the beer.*

*Henry VIII had an *abbess on his knee*, which made walking difficult.

Humor in Spoonerism

It's an error in speech or deliberate play on words in which corresponding consonants, vowels, or morphemes are switched.

*"Half-formed wish" becomes "*I have been nursing a half-warmed fish.*"

*"The bridegroom kissed the bride and cussed the maid" becomes "*The bridegroom kissed the maid and cussed the bride.*"

*"Sir, you have wasted two whole terms; you have missed all my history lectures and you have been caught lighting a fire in the quad; you will leave Oxford by the next down train." It comes out of the Rev. W. A. Spooner (1844-1930), Warden of New College, Oxford, this way: *"Sir, you have tasted two whole worms; you have hissed all my mystery lectures and you have been caught fighting a liar in the quad; you will leave Oxford by next town train."*

Humor in Howlers of the Press

*Most people know the position assumed by the present recumbent. But where will he stand when he takes his seat?

*It is with real regret that we learn of Mr. Wayne's recovery from an automobile accident.

*Criminal jury dismissed.

*Hamm fails to identify Yeggs.

*Maddened steer injured farmer with Ax.

*The fatal accident occurred at the corner of Broadway and Fourth Street just as the dead man attempted to cross.

*Why go elsewhere to be cheated? You can come to us to do the job.

*"Family catches fire just in time," chief says.

*Grandmother of fourteen shoots hole in one.

*Hospital sued eight foot doctors.

Humor in One-line Zingers

*The closest to perfection a person ever comes is when he fills out a job application. (Stanley Randall)

*Cricket is the only game that you can actually put on weight when playing. (Tommy Docherty)

*He pursued his studies but never overtook them. (H. G. Wells)

*If you don't know where you are going, any road will take you there. (Lewis Caroll)

*William Pitt was stiff with everyone but the ladies. (Percy Bysshe Shelley)

*You look at Ernest Borgnine and you think to yourself: Was anybody else hurt in the accident? (Don Rickles)

*A graceful taunt is worth a thousand insults. (Louis Nizer)

*A man can't be too careful in the choice of his enemies. (Oscar Wilde)

*A narcissist is someone better-looking than you are. (Gore Vidal)

*Altruism is a fine motive, but if you want results, greed works much better. (Herbert Spencer)

*Don't be humble. You're not that great. (Golda Meir)

*Don't mistake pleasure for happiness. They're a different breed of dog. (Josh Billings)

*Even if you're on the right track, you'll get run over if you just sit there. (Will Rogers)

*Given enough time, what you put off doing today will eventually get done by itself. (G. Gestra)

*Glory is fleeting but obscurity is forever. (Napoleon Bonaparte)

*Experience is a good teacher, but the fees are high. (Heinrich Heine)

*Good judgment comes from experience, and experience comes from bad judgment. (Barry LePatner)

*Great spirits have always encountered violent opposition from mediocre minds. (Albert Einstein)

*Happiness isn't something you experience; it's something you remember. (Oscar Levant)

*Having it all doesn't necessarily mean having it all at once. (Stephanie Luetkehans)

*Honest criticism is hard to take, especially from a relative, a friend, an acquaintance, or a stranger. (Franklin P. Jones)

*Honesty is the best policy—when there is money in it. (Mark Twain)

*I agree with what you say, but I will kill you if you say it again. (Alan S. Watt)

*I am a great believer in luck, and I find the harder I work the more I have of it. (Stephen Leacock)

*I am not young enough to know everything. (James Mathew Barrie)

*I don't think adversity necessarily builds character, but it certainly gives you an opportunity to display it. (Gary Bean)

*If you want truly to understand something, try to change it. (Kurt Lewin)

*In baiting a mousetrap with cheese, always leave room for the mouse. (Hector Hugo Munro)

*In the long run we are all dead. (John Maynard Keynes)

*Inferiority is what you enjoy in your best friends. (Lord Chesterfield)

*It has been my experience that folks who have no vices have very few virtues. (Abraham Lincoln)

*It is a funny thing about life; if you refuse to accept anything but the best, you very often get it. (W. Somerset Maugham)

*It is better to go into a corner slow and come out fast, than go in fast and come out dead. (Sterling Moss)

*It is not the thing we like to do, but liking the thing we have to do that makes life blessed. (Goethe)

*It is not true that life is one damn thing after another—it is one damn thing over and over. (Edna St. Vincent Millay)

*It is better to waste one's youth than to do nothing with it at all. (Georges Courteline)

*Let us so live that when we come to die even the undertaker will be sorry. (Mark Twain)

*Life is a comedy to those who think and a tragedy to those who feel. (Voltaire)

*Man is the only animal that blushes or needs to. (Mark Twain)

*Nature has given two ears but only one mouth. (Benjamin Disraeli)

*Nearly all men can stand adversity, but if you want to test a man's character, give him power. (Abraham Lincoln)

*No innocent man buys a gun, and no happy man writes his memoirs. (Garrison Keillor)

*No one can make you feel inferior without your consent. (Eleanor Roosevelt)

*Nothing is good or bad but by comparison. (Thomas Fuller)

*Obstacles are things a person sees when he takes his eyes off his goal. (E. Joseph Cossman)

*One should forgive one's enemies but not before they are hanged. (Heinrich Heine)

*People are lonely because they build walls instead of bridges. (Joseph F. Newton)

*People who bite the hand that feeds them usually lick the boot that kicks them. (Eric Hoffer)

*Perseverance is not a long race; it is many short races one after the other. (Walter Elliott)

*Sometimes the poorest man leaves his children the richest inheritance. (Ruth E. Renkel)

*Every man has a right to be stupid, but comrade Macdonald abuses the privilege. (Leon Trotsky)

*The key to ambition is the ability to cloak it. (Maureen Dowd)

*Fleas can be taught nearly anything that a Congressman can. (Mark Twain)

*Do not do unto others as you would that they should do unto you. Their tastes may not be the same. (Bernard Shaw)

*I know why the sun never sets on the British Empire: God wouldn't trust an Englishman in the dark. (Duncan Spaeth)

*American women expect to find in their husbands the perfection that English women only hope to find in their butlers. (W. Somerset Maugham)

*The thing that impresses me most about America is the way parents obey their children. (W. Somerset Maugham)

*I don't even know what street Canada is on. (Al Capone)

*What kills a skunk is the publicity it gives itself. (Abraham Lincoln)

*When I called him an SOB, I am not using profanity but am referring to the circumstances of his birth. (Governor Huey Long of Louisiana on the Imperial Wizard of the Ku Klux Klan)

*Dewey has thrown his diaper into the ring. (Harold L. Ickes)

*The Right Honorable Gentleman is indebted to his memory for his jests and to his imagination for his facts. (Richard Brinsley Sheridan on the Earl of Dundas)

*Sweet praise is like perfume. It's fine if you don't swallow it. (Dwight Eisenhower)

Humor in My Collection of Amusing Sound Bites

*Reader, suppose you were an idiot and suppose you were a member of Congress: I repeat myself.

*I did not listen because I have a baby of my own.

*It's easier to suffer in silence if you're sure someone is watching.

*It's a small world. So you gotta use your elbows a lot.

*It was so cold the politicians had their hands in their own pockets.

*Eating vegetables is much crueler than eating animals. At least animals have a chance to run away.

*The play was so bad I asked the woman in front to put her hat on.

*Some days you are the pigeon. Some days you are the statue.

*I enjoyed the speech, although I was sorry to miss my children growing up.

*What's the death rate around here? Same as everywhere else, one per person.

*If you tell the truth, you don't have to remember anything.

*When you are arguing with an idiot try to make sure he isn't doing the same thing.

*Advice to public speakers—if you don't strike oil within two minutes, stop boring.

*To make a long story short, there's nothing like having the boss walk in.

*A young doctor means a new graveyard.

*As long as you've lit a candle, you're allowed to curse the darkness.

*As my grandfather used to say, "If we all liked the same thing, the world would be after your grandma."

*Don't ask a barber whether you need a haircut.

*Anthony's Law of Force: Don't force it—get a big hammer.

*Faith may move mountains, but it was the whip that built the pyramids.

*He promised me earrings, but he only pierced my ears.

*His absence is good company.

*I know very few ideas worth dying for, none worth killing for.

*If a man says to you, "It isn't the money; it's the principle of the thing," I'll lay you six to one it's the money.

*If you look around the table and can't tell who the sucker is, it's you.

*It is easier to wear slippers than to carpet the entire world.

*It only takes a little bit of greed to get a whole lot of stuff.

*Laugh and the world laughs with you; cry and the world laughs at you or you get wet.

*Left over nuts never match left over bolts.

*Remember, amateurs built the ark. Professionals built the Titanic.

*No matter how thin you slice it, it's still baloney.

*No problem is so large that it can't be fit in somewhere.

*Speak the truth, but leave immediately after.

*Today's peacock is tomorrow's feather duster.

Humor in Paradox

It is a statement or group of statements that leads to a contradiction or a situation which defies logic or reason.

*This narrative is considered one of the greatest paradoxes ever recorded in history—an excellent teaser.

Many years ago, a law professor came across a clever student who was eager to become an attorney but did not have the means to pay for the course. The student struck a deal saying, "I would pay your fee the day I win my first case in court." The professor agreed and paid for the course. The student now was a full-fledged attorney. However, he paid scant attention to the deal and was making no attempt to pay up. Any amount of pestering by the professor for his money fell deaf on the young attorney's ears. Fed up, the professor decided to sue for the repayment of his debt in a court of law. They both were going to argue the case for themselves.

And this is how the two saw his chances of winning.

The professor: If I win this case, as per court of law, student has to pay me. And if I lose the case, the student has to still pay me because he would have won his first case. So either way, I will get my money.

The student: If I win this case, as per court of law, I don't have to pay anything to the professor. And if I lose the case, I don't have to pay him because I haven't won my first case yet. So either way I am not going to pay the professor anything.

*God is omnipotent (all-powerful) which means there is nothing God can't do.

So can God build a mountain so large he can't move it?

If yes, then he *can't* move it.

If no, then He *can't* create it.

Either way, there is something He cannot do (therefore a paradox).

*A prisoner is told, "You will die within ten days on a day that you will not be expecting it."

Well, it cannot be the tenth day, because if he will die within ten days, and he is alive on the tenth day, he will expect to die on that day.

Since he cannot die on the tenth day (see above), he cannot die on the ninth day either. Since he cannot die on the tenth day, if the ninth day comes, he will be expecting it.

Likewise, he cannot die on the eighth day or the seventh day, etc., all the way to the first day.

*You must make a statement. If it is true, I will choke you to death. If it is false, your head shall be cut off.

Answer: My head shall be cut off.

If this is true, then you will be choked to death, which makes it false.

Humor in Using One Word too Many

*Free of charge

*Beverage items

*Sting operation

*Facial area

*Daily basis

*Blue in color

*Shooting incident

Humor in Using Code Words

There has never been an age as wary as ours of the tricks words can play, obscuring distinctions and smoothing over the corrugations of the actual word. (Geoffrey Nurenberg)

It has become everyday parlance for especially politicians regardless of pigmentation, indifferent conservatives, and incurable liberals or inflexible "Tea Partiers" to use words often with insidious intent to conjure up in the minds of listeners more than what the words purport to mean playing Trojan horse with words, kind of linguistic dog whistles. (Don't say "nigger," say "forced busing," "states' rights," and "food stamp recipents.") However, if we look at these words with critical detachment, we will be able to see the humor in them. To list a few examples:

*Islamo-fascism.

*We do not torture.

*Palling around with terrorists.

*Socialized medicine.

*The pro-America areas of this great nation.

*Christian right.

*The decider.

*People of faith.

*"Abu-Grab-Ass."

*Family values.

*Enhanced interrogation techniques.

*Liberal media.

Humor in Dry or Deadpan Humor

It's characterized by a calm and straight forward delivery with a deadpan look.

*I am so broke I cannot afford to pay attention.

*It sounds like English, but I cannot understand a word you're saying.

*How about never? Is never good for you?

**My late husband was Irish and had an extremely dry sense of humor.

I once told him that a man, passing me in the street, said to me, "Hello gorgeous."

My husband replied, with a straight face, "What color was his guide dog?"

**My old neighbor Gramp Wiley was not too pleased when he heard that my friend Winky got a job as an ambulance driver. He said, "Winky can't work on that ambulance. Winky is stupid. He gets everything back end to. It would be just my luck to have Winky show up in that ambulance at two o'clock some morning when I'm lying here on the kitchen floor needing a tube shoved down my throat."

Humor in Billboards

*Myrtle Beach has seven hundred restaurants. There goes your diet.

*Ace Hardware: "Need a good screw?"

*Ray Ban: "We'd love to be sitting on your face."

*FedEx: "We'd love to handle your package."

*Ikea: "Come, check out our stool samples."

*Hammond: "We're proud of our organs."

*North American Fertilizer Association: "You think your job involves a lot of bullshit?"

Humor in Dialect Humor

Not all humor evokes sidesplitting laughter. Sometimes it produces a wry and bitter smile.

Nothing in the world is quite funny as the mispronunciations and hamstrung syntax of various ethnic groups—whether they are Italians, South Asians, Chinese, or any other. Mark Twain used to great effect different dialects in Tom Sawyer and Huckleberry Finn.

Chinese

A man having given his pants to the dry cleaners goes to collect it but had lost the receipt. Here is what he is told by the proprietor:

"All samee. No tickee, no washee, no shirtee. You bling tickee, you catchem washee."

Mexican

"My wife gets mad and I don't even know *water* problem is."

"Yo,' when all my familia gets in the car, there's not *mushroom*."

"Ju tol me ju were going to the store and *july* me. *Julyer.*"

"Hey man, I'm looking for Paco, tell me if *juicy* him."

Indian

A Sikh walked into a travel agency in New Delhi and said to an agent, "I wish to purchase an airplane ticket to the Netherlands. I must go to the *Haig-you.*"

"Oh, you foolish Sikh, not *Haig-you*. You mean the "*The Hague.*"

"I am the customer. You hold your *tung-you.*"

"My my, you really are quite illiterate," laughed the agent. "It is not *tung-you*. It is *tongue.*"

"Just sell me the ticket, you cheeky fellow. I am not here to *arg.*"

Humor in Medical Indecision

*Four doctors went duck hunting together. Together in the duck blind, they decided that instead of all shooting away at the same time, they would take turns as each duck came by. The first to have a shot would be the general practitioner, next would be the internist, then the surgeon, and finally the pathologist.

When the first bird flew over, the general practitioner lifted his shotgun, but never fired, saying, "I am not sure that was a duck."

The second bird was the internist's. He aimed and followed the bird in his sights, saying, "It looks like a duck, it flies like a duck, it sounds like a duck . . ." but then the bird was out of range, and the internist didn't take a shot.

As soon as the third appeared flying up out of the water, only a few feet from the blind, the surgeon blasted away emptying his pump gun and blowing the bird to smithereens. Turning to the pathologist, the surgeon said, "Go see whether that was a duck."

*A man subject to epileptic seizure was picked up unconscious on the streets of New York and rushed to a hospital, and when they took off his coat, one of the nurses found a piece of paper pinned to the lining, upon which was written, "To inform the house surgeon that this is just a case of plain fit—not appendicitis. My appendix has been removed twice."

Humor in Relational Reversal

Here humor is when roles are reversed. Relational Reversal is a very common gambit in humorous newspaper columns. The following is a very good example.

*A marquis at the court of Louis XIV enters his wife's bedroom and finds her in the arms of the bishop. He sees them and walks calmly to the window and goes through the motions of blessing the people in the street.

"What are you doing?" cries the perplexed wife.

"Well, the bishop is doing my job, so I decided to do his."

Humor in Homonyms

They are words that have the same pronunciation or spelling but different meanings.

*I enjoy *bass fishing* and playing the *bass guitar.*

*He who jumps off a bridge in Paris is *in Seine.*

*A man's home is his castle, in a *manor* of speaking.

*Reading while sunbathing makes you *well red.*

No dogs are allowed here. Don't you *know* that?

*There will be no *peace* in this house if someone ate the last *piece* of Dad's birthday cake.

*The children need your *presence* more than your *presents.*

Humor in Homophones

They are words which have the same pronunciation as each other but different spelling and meanings.

*They went and *told the sexton* and the *sexton toll'd the bell.*

*I *know* the right answer. *No,* you don't.

*Do you have *some* boxes? I have a big *sum* of cash to put in.

*The *band* was *banned* from playing.

Humor in Homograph

They are words which are spelt the same as each other but which have a different meaning.

*The professor was *reading an abstract* about *abstract art.*

*The tiger was so *close* I had to *close* the door.

*The diver *dove* into the pool with barely a splash as the *dove* cooed at the passers-by.

Humor in Figures of Speech

Anaphora: beginning consecutive phrases with same word.

*I needed a drink.

I needed a lot of life insurance.

I needed a vacation.

I needed a home in the county.

What I had was a coat, a hat and a gun.

(Raymond Chandler, *Farewell, My Lovely*, 1940)

Humor in Aposiopesis

It is stopping in midsentence and letting the listener complete the thought.

*"Almira Gulch, just because you own half the country, doesn't mean that you have the power to run the rest of us. For twenty-three years, I've been dying to tell you what I thought of you! And now . . . well, being a Christian woman, I can't say it."

*That all the world shall—I will do things—

What they are yet, I know not, but they shall be

The terrors of the earth!

(William Shakespeare, *King Lear*)

*"I won't sleep in the same bed with a woman who thinks I'm lazy! I'm going downstairs, unfold the couch, unroll the sleeping ba . . . uh, goodnight." (Homer Simpson in *The Simpsons*)

*"Dear Ketel One Drinker—There comes a time in everyone's life when they just want to stop what they're doing and . . ." (Print ad for Ketel One Vodka, 2007)

Humor in Paraprosdokian Figure of Speech

It's a figure of speech where the final words make the reader see the first part of the sentence in a new light.

*I asked God for a bike, but I know God doesn't work that way, so I stole a bike and asked for forgiveness.

*Do not argue with an idiot; he will drag you down to his level and beat you with experience.

*The last thing I want to do is hurt you, but it's still on the list.

*Light travels faster than sound; this is why some people appear bright until you hear them speak.

*If I agreed with you we'd both be wrong.

*We never really grow up; we only learn how to act in public.

*If you are supposed to learn from your mistakes, why do some people have more than one child?

*War does not determine who is right—only who is left.

*Knowledge is knowing tomato is a fruit; wisdom is not putting it in a fruit salad.

*The early bird might get the worm, but the second mouse gets the cheese.

*A bus station is where a bus stops. A train station is where a train stops. On my desk, I have a work station.

*How is it one careless match can start a forest fire? But it takes a whole box to start a campfire.

*A bank is a place that will lend you money, if you can prove that you don't need it.

*I didn't say it was your fault, I said I was blaming you.

*Why does someone believe you when you say there are four billion stars, but they have to check when you say the paint is wet?

*Why do Americans choose from just two people to run for president and fifty for Miss America?

*Behind every successful man is his woman. Behind the fall of a successful man is usually another woman.

Humor in Haiku

Haiku are like limericks. They are short poems with a certain number of lines. Haiku poems date from the ninth century Japan to the present day. It is more than a type of poem; it is a way of looking at the physical world and seeing something deeper, like the very nature of existence.

*Make up your mind, snail!

You are half inside your house,

And halfway out!

*Shut up, you crickets!

How can I hear what my wife

Is saying to me?"

You moths must leave now;

I am turning out the light

And going to sleep.

*"Oh, Mr. Scarecrow,

Stop waving your arms about

Like a foreigner."

*The day is long

That even noisy sparrows

Fall silent.

*Even toy soldiers

Perspire with weariness

In the autumn mist.

*I almost forgot

To hang up an autumn moon

Over the mountain.

*They smelt like roses;

But when I put on the light,

They were violets.

*A freezing morning:
I left a bit of my skin
On the broomstick handle.

*A balmy spring wind
Reminding me something
I cannot recall.

*I feel autumn rain
Trying to explain something
I do not want to know.

*A sleepless spring night:
Yearning for what I never had,
And for what never was.

*How lonely it is:
A winter world full of rain,
Rain raining on rain.

*In a drizzling rain,
In a flower shop's doorway,
A girl sells herself.

*A nude fat woman

Stands over a kitchen stove,

Tasting applesauce.

*I am paying rent

For the ice in my cold room

And the moonlight too.

*Two flies locked in love

Were hit by a newspaper

And died together.

*It is September,

The month in which I was born;

And I have no thoughts.

*With its first blossom,

The little apple tree brags:

"Look, look! Me too!"

*It's so hot that

The scarecrow has taken off

*Even while sleeping;

The scabby little puppy

Scratches his fleas.

*Sadly, the only
Guy I'm going steady with
Is my bartender.

*Whenever I spot
A cool pair of shoes, attached
Is an Asian chick.

*It turns out staring
Is a great way to seduce
(narcissistic) men.

*It would appear that
My biological clock
Has a snooze button.

*I saw an old flame
And he looked. Just terrible.
Ah, schadenfreude.

*A kiss on the hand
May be quite continental . . .
Buy me dinner first.

*I like trysts with guys
From other countries. It's like
Stamping your passport.

*Construction workers:
Unfairly stereotyped?
I hear no catcalls.

*From random street guy
The best pickup line ever:
"I'll make you breakfast!"

*Men don't realize
We women thrill to conquest
As much as they do.

*His proposition:
"Let's make out like teenagers!"
How could I refuse?"

*He makes me happy.
If he also makes me sad,
Then I'll know it's love.

*As I get older,

I can hear all of my "whens"

Transform into "ifs."

Humor in Southern Dialect

Southern expressions are those vivid, wonderful similes, metaphors, or other sayings that are used on a regular basis during conversations in the South.

*So bucktoothed he could eat corn-on-the-cob through a key hole.

*So poor he'd have to borrow money to buy water to cry with.

*Older than the mountains and got twice as much dust.

*That's a gracious plenty (when being offered something).

*Crazier than a run over dog.

*Tougher than a one eared alley cat.

*Scared my mule (when something really startled them).

*So ugly she'd run a dog off a meat wagon.

*As scarce as hen's teeth.

*Done gone and got Yankee rich.

*Sorry as a two-dollar watch.

*Plumb tuckered out.

*Full as a tick.

*Fat as a tub o' lard.

*In all my born days . . .

Chunk: To throw. "Chunk it there, Leroy. Ole Leroy sure can chunk 'at ball, can't he? Best pitcher we ever had."

Dollin: Another term of endearment (darling) "Dollin, will you marry me?"

Dreckly: Soon. "He'll be along dreckly."

Everhoo: Another baffling Southernism—a reverse contraction of who-ever. "Everhoo one of you kids wants to go to the movie better clean up their room."

Fahn: Excellent. "That sure is a fahn-lookin' woman."

Farn: Anything that is not domestic. "Ah don't drink that farn liquor, specially Rooshin vodka."

Fetchin': Attractive. "That's a mighty fetchin' woman. I think I'll ask her to daints."

Gammut: A large institution operating out of Wasington that consumes taxes at a fearful rate. "Bill's got it made. He's got a gammut job."

Hush yo' mouth: An expression of pleased embarrassment, as when a Southern female is paid an extravagant compliment. "Honey, you're 'bout the sweetest, best—lookin' woman in Tennessee. Now hush yo' mouth, Jim Bob."

Jackleg: Self-taught, especially in reference to automobile mechanics and clergymen. "He's just a jackleg preacher, but he sure knows how to put out the hellfire and brimstone."

Kerosene cat in hell with gasoline drawers on: A colorful Southern expression used as evaluation of someone's ability to accomplish something. "He ain't got no more chance than a kerosene cat in hell with gasoline drawers on."

Lick and a promise: To do something in a hurried or perfunctory fashion. "We don't have time to clean this house so it's spotless. Just give it a lick and a promise."

Ownliest: The only one. "That's the ownliest one ah've got left."

Yontny: Do you want any. "Yonty more cornbread?"

Exclamation: "Well, knock me down and steal muh teeth."

Threat: "I'll slap you so hard, your clothes will be outtastyle."

Compliment: Cute as a sack full of puppies

The weather: "It's so dry the trees are bribing the dogs."

*You look about as happy as a tick on a fat dog.

*She was so tall if she fell down she would be halfway home.

*Don't you piss on my leg and tell me it's raining.

*You're lying like a no-legged dog

*Excuses are like backsides. Everybody's got one and they all stink.

*She could make a preacher cuss.

*Each one of his sermons is better than the next.

*He's so useless if he had a third hand he would need another pocket to put it in.

*That boy's more slippery than snot on a glass doorknob.

*He's about as handy as a back pocket on a shirt.

*She's so clumsy she could trip over a cordless phone.

*He's about as useful as a pogo stick in quicksand.

*Well, slap my head and call me silly.

*He's so dumb he could throw himself on the ground and miss.

*He squeezes a quarter so tight the eagle screams.

*He doesn't have a pot to pee in or a window to throw it out.

*She's so ugly; I'd hire her to haunt a house.

Descriptions

*A bothersome person is "like a booger that you can't thump off."

*When something is bad, then you say, "That ain't no count."

*"He ran like his feet was on fire, and his ass was catchin."

*Your momma's so fat, when she stepped up on the scale to be weighed, it said, "To be continued."

*Any insulting statement is always followed by "bless his or her heart."

Example: "She's dumber than a doorknob, bless her heart."

Humor in Black Slang

From *Titters* edited by Deanne Stillman and Anne Beatts.

Much of black slang passes quickly into the language of the white community through the process known as "ripping off."

Abbadabba honeymoon: A blind date set up so that two extremely ugly people can meet. Arranging such dates is considered a right-on thing to do.

Bad: Formerly meant good. Now means bad or good.

Bleach: Bribe money.

Down home: Formerly meant the South. Now means the Manhattan House of Detention (also known as the "Tombs").

Get metroed (from Metropolitan Life): To be discovered hiding in the closet just after your kid has told the insurance man you weren't at home.

James Brown someone: To grab a person and process his hair against his will. An act of political punishment for those who act too "white." If the person is so reactionary, he already has a process, he is *Goldberged*—that is, held underwater until his hair kinks up again reminding him of his roots.

Job hunting: Sleeping or messing up on your job so persistently that you are fired and therefore have to look for employment elsewhere.

Junior jumper: A rapist under sixteen years of age.

Kip (short for Kipling): Welfare money.

Let me fry your eggs: Let me scramble your brains. Tell you some startling news.

MCP: (Originally stood for "my Cadillac payment.") By extension, it is now used for anything that has the highest priority.

Owens (sing. & pl.): A roach or roaches. Named after Olympic track star Jesse Owens because they're brown and they are quick.

Parasol: A black person who is passing for white.

Rufus: The name being held in reserve for the first all-black state.

Tough maracas: Depending on voice pitch, either the highest compliment or the grossest insult that can be directed at those of Hispanic descent.

Wishbone: Money, loot, or bread. You have to have money. Wishing won't cut it.

Humor in Funny Redneck Sayings and Quotes

Redneck is a historically derogatory slang term used in reference to poor, uneducated white farmers, especially from the Southern United States.

*He fell out of the ugly tree and hit every branch on the way down.

*She was so ugly she could trick or treat over the telephone.

*Darlin', you're hotter than donut grease at a fat man convention.

*Busier than a one-legged man in an ass-kickin contest.

*Well, butter my butt and call me biscuit.

*That boy is about as sharp as a cue ball.

*Can't swing a dead cat without hitting a Walmart.

*It's hotter than the hinges of hell.

*Well, she's finer than a frog hair split eight ways.

Humor in Funny Hillbilly Slang

Hillbilly is a term referring to certain people who dwell in rural, mountainous areas of the United States, primarily Appalachia but also the Ozarks. The term is frequently considered derogatory, and so is usually offensive to those of Americans of Appalachian heritage.

*Not worth a hoot and a holler.

*Don't let it rattle your bones.

**Pert neer, but not plumb.

*The chitlins are out playin' in the sandbox.

**If I was any better I'd be twins.

*Busier than a cat burying poop.

*That's like pushing a watermelon through a garden hose.

*Hit him so hard it killed his relatives.

*Knocked him into next week.

*Older than Methuselah.

*Time to shit or get off the pot.

*Like white on rice.

*Two can live as cheap as one if one don't eat.

**Dropped him like a bad habit.

*So tight he squeaks when he walks.

Ripley's Believe It or Not

Message in a Bottle

William T. Mullen's wife warned him that if he didn't stop drinking, she would humiliate him after his death. He paid no attention and died in 1863, whereupon she carried out her threat by giving him a gravestone—at Clayton, Alabama—in the shape of a whiskey bottle.

Snail Mail

A letter sent to the German town of Ostheim vor der Rhön in 1718 arrived in 2004, surviving 286 years in the postal system. *That's how reliable the postal service is.*

Silent Mourning

Women of the Warramunga tribe of Australia do not speak for a year after the death of their husbands—communicating instead only with hand and arm gestures.

Easier than ABC

Rotokas, a language of the South Pacific, has an alphabet with only eleven letters, comprising six consonants and five vowels.

Wrist-breaker

That K. S. Raghavendra, from India, is capable of breaking thirteen eggs in thirty seconds. It doesn't sound amazing in itself, except that he doesn't break them by clenching his fist, but by bending his hand back over his wrist.

Tallest Man

When Robert Wadlow died in 1940, at the age of twenty-two, he was 8 feet 11 inches tall, weighed 440 pounds, wore a size 37 AA shoe, and had a 25 ring size.

Internet Marathon

In November 1997, Canada's Daniel Messier spent 103 hours nonstop surfing the Internet—that's more than four days.

Baby Driver

When his three-year-old cousin was hurt in a fall in 2005, Tanishk Boyas drove him straight to hospital. Nothing unusual in that—except that Tanishk was only five at the time! The youngster had been learning to drive for three months at his home in India, but when he climbed into the family van, it was the first time he had driven it without adult supervision. His father said, "He used to watch me drive and grasped the basics."

Living Library

In 2005, instead of lending books, a library in Malmo, Sweden, lent out humans. In an attempt to overcome common prejudices, borrowers were able to take the human items, including a homosexual, a journalist, and a blind person for a forty-five minute-chat in the library's outdoor café.

Poetic Justice

After two US thieves stole a checkbook from the home of Mr. and Mrs. David Conner, they went to a bank with a $200 check made out to themselves. The female teller asked them to wait a minute and then called security. The teller was Mrs. David Conner.

Humor in Caricature

Some of the earliest caricatures are found in the works of Leonardo da Vinci who actively sought people with deformities to use as models. The point was to offer an impression of the original which was more striking than a portrait.

Caricature in literature is a description of a person using exaggeration of some characteristics and over simplification of others in order to impress upon the reader. We will be able to understand caricature if we compare caricature to cartoon. According to Indian cartoonist S. Jithesh, "a caricature is the satire illustration of a person or a thing. But a cartoon is the satirical illustration of an idea."

*Charles Dickens delighted in the use of caricatures in his novels. Here is a well-known example in *Bleak House*. "Mr. Chadband is a large yellow man, with a fat smile, and a general appearance of having a good deal of train oil in his system. Mrs. Chadband is a stern, severe-looking, silent woman. Mr. Chadband moves softly and cumbrously, not unlike a bear who has been taught to walk upright. He is very much embarrassed about the arms, as if they were inconvenient to him, and he wanted to grovel; is very much in a perspiration about the head; and never speaks without first putting up his great hand, as delivering a token to his hearers that he is going to edify them."

*George Orwell in his *Animal Farm* caricatures prominent personalities of the Russian Revolution. Mr. Jones is Tsar Nicholas II, the farm itself is Russia, the neighboring farms are neighboring countries (particularly Pinchfield, representing

Germany, and Foxwood, representing the allies), old Major is Marx (with perhaps a bit of Lenin), Napoleon as mentioned is Stalin, Snowball is Trotsky and Squealer is Pravda and the Russian government propaganda in general.

Humor in Mondegreen

They are instances where something is misheard and then misinterpreted.

*"I led the pigeons to the flag" for ("I pledge allegiance to the flag").

*"Excuse me while I kiss this guy" (in the Jimi Hendrix lyric, "Excuse Me while I Kiss the Sky.")

*"The ants are my friends" (for "The answer, my friend," in "Blowing in the Wind," by Bob Dylan.)

*"Take your pants down, and make it happen" (for "Take your passion and make it happen" in Irene Cara's *Flashdance*.)

*"Every time you go away/you take a piece of meat with you" (for " . . . take a piece of me with you," from the Paul Young song "Every Time You Go Away.")

*Consecrated cross-eyed bear (for "A consecrated cross I bear.")

Humor in Farce

It is a comedy which aims at entertaining the audience by means of unlikely, extravagant, and improbable situations, verbal humor of varying degrees of sophistication, including wordplay.

Classic example: Oscar Wilde's "The Importance of Being Earnest," which is considered the best verbal farce ever written.

*The play is based around two young men: one is an upright young man called Jack who lives in the country. However, in order to escape the drudgery of his highly conservative lifestyle, he has created an alter ego, Ernest, who has all kinds of unsavory fun in London. Jack says he often has to visit his poor brother Ernest, which gives him an opportunity to escape his boring life and have fun with his good friend, Algernon.

However, Algernon comes to suspect that Jack is leading a double life when he finds a personal message in one of Jack's cigarette cases. Jack now makes a clean breast of his life, including the fact that he has a young and attractive guardian by the name Cecily Cardew back in his estate in Gloucestershire. This peeks Algenon's interest and, uninvited, he turns up on the estate pretending to be Jack's brother—the reprobate Ernest—in order to woe Cecily. In the meantime, Jack's fiancé, Gwendolen, has also arrived, and Jack admits to her that he is, in fact, not called Ernest but is called Jack. Algernon, despite his better judgment, also confesses to Cecily that his name is not Ernest either. These misunderstandings and entanglements produce a great deal of farcical humor.

Humor in Insults

It is where every sentence buzzes with malice or drips with venom.

The ancient Romans were never afraid to be uncomplimentary; the poet Martial made a career of it.

*I could do without your face, Chloe, and without your neck, and your hands, and your limbs, and to save myself the trouble of mentioning the points in detail, I could do without you altogether. (Marcus Valerius Martial)

*Sir Edward Coke to Sir Walter Raleigh:

I will prove you the notoriousest traitor that ever came to the bar . . . thou art a monster; thou hast an English face, but a Spanish heart . . . Thou art the most vile and execrable traitor that ever lived . . . I want words sufficient to express thy viperous treasons. Thou art an odious fellow; thy name is hateful to all the realm of England . . . There never lived a viler viper upon the face of the earth than thou.

*The gentle Charles Lamb suffered the sad fate of many a playwright when his new play was hissed on its first night. So violent was the audience's reaction that Lamb joined in the hissing himself, lest he be mistaken for the author! Describing the scene to a friend, the mild Lamb later unleashed an uncharacteristic torrent of venom:

Mercy on us, that God should give his favorite children, men, mouths to speak with discourse rationally, to promise smoothly, to flatter agreeably, to encourage warmly, to counsel wisely: to sing with, to drink with, and to kiss with: and that they should turn them into mouths of adders, bears, wolves, hyenas, and whistle like tempests, and emit breath through them like distillations of aspic poison, to asperse and vilify the innocent labor of their fellow creatures who are desirous to please the . . . God be pleased to make the breath stink and the teeth rot out of them all therefore. (Charles Lamb)

*He's a little man, that's his trouble. Never trust a man with short legs—brains too near their bottoms. (Noel Coward)

*The traditional gypsy curse:

May you wander over the face of the earth forever, never sleep twice in the same bed, never drink water twice from the same well, and never cross the same river twice in a year.

*Ralph Waldo Emerson on poet William Wordsworth:

"Is Wordsworth a bell with a wooden tongue?"

*Harry S. Truman to *Washington Post* music critic Paul Hume:

I have just read your lousy review buried in the back pages. You sound like a frustrated old man who never made a success, an eight-ulcer man on a four-ulcer job, and all four ulcers working. I have never met you, but if I do you'll need a new nose and plenty of beefsteak and perhaps a supporter below.

*Thomas Carlyle on Charles Lamb:

Charles Lamb, I sincerely believe you to be in some considerable degree insane. A more pitiful, rickety, gasping, staggering, stammering Tomfool I do not know.

*Thomas Carlyle once refused to receive the poet Swinburne on the grounds that he had no wish to meet someone who was *sitting in a sewer and adding to it.*

*Dr. Samuel Johnson on Thomas Sheridan:

Why, sir, Sherry is dull, naturally dull; but it must have taken him a great deal of pains to become what we now see him. Such excess of stupidity, sir, is not in nature.

*Virginia Woolf on James Joyce:

The work of queasy undergraduate scratching his pimples.

*Senator Reed Smoot on James Joyce:

It is written by a man with a diseased mind and soul so black that he would even obscure the darkness of hell.

*D. H. Lawrence to Katherine Mansfield:

I loathe you. You revolt me stewing on your consumption . . . The Italians were quite right to have nothing to do with you.

*D. H. Lawrence on Katherine Mansfield and J. Middleton Murray:

Spit on her for me when you see her; she's a liar out and out. As for him, I reserve my language . . . Vermin, the pair of 'em.

*D. H. Lawrence's characteristic attitude was one of rage against all dolts who would not appreciate him:

Curse the blasted, jelly-boned swines, the slimy, the belly-wriggling invertebrates, the miserable sodding rotters, the flaming sods, the sniveling, dribbling, dithering, palsied, pulseless lot that make up England today. They've got white of egg in their veins, and their spunk is that watery it's a marvel they can breed. They can do nothing but frog-spawn—the gibberers! God, how I hate them!

Samuel Johnson has been called "the master of the put-down." Here's a selection from Jack Lynch's *Samuel Johnson's Insults.*

*Woman: Why, Doctor, I believe you prefer the company of men to that of ladies.

Johnson: Madam, I am very fond of the company of ladies; I like their beauty, I like their delicacy, I like their vivacity, and I like their silence.

*Often Johnson would grow exasperated with a sparring partner who thought too highly of himself. When, in the midst of a dispute, one opponent said, "I don't understand you, sir." Johnson rejoined, "Sir, I have found you an argument, but I am not obliged to find you an understanding."

*Boswell, for all his charm, could be annoying. Sometimes Johnson found him too much to take. One night he asked too many questions, prompting Johnson to spit out, "Sir, you have but two topics, yourself and me. I am sick of both."

*When a Scottish friend insisted "Scotland had a great many noble wild prospects," Johnson agreed that there were beautiful prospects aplenty, "But, sir, let me tell you, the noblest prospect which a Scotsman ever sees is the high road that leads him to England."

*Even more fun than ridiculing Scotland was ridiculing the Scots. "The impudence of an Irishman is the impudence of a fly, that buzzes about you and you put it away, but it returns again, and flutters and teases you. The impudence of a Scotsman is the impudence of a leech that fixes and sucks your blood."

*When the young Sam misbehaved, his mother called him a puppy. The son's reply? "I asked her if she knew what they called a puppy's mother?"

*A fiddler didn't have to be "vile" to earn Johnson's scorn. While he sat bored through a concert, a friend whispered to him that the famous violinist was performing a very difficult piece. "Difficult do you call it, sir? I wish it were impossible."

*And though he adored Shakespeare, he could raise hackles by criticizing even the bard: "Shakespeare never has six lines together without a fault."

Humor in Trivia

The expression has come to suggest information of the kind useful almost exclusively for answering "quiz" questions—hence the brand name trivial pursuit.

*According to Greek historians, kissing began when, menfolk wanted to know if their womenfolk had been sipping wine. A kiss on the lips could give a clue.

*The Japanese do not bathe to wash away dirt. They do that before they enter the tub. The bath in Japan is a social experience, a time for the family and any close friends who happen to be present to climb into the water together, to relax, gossip, argue, and laugh.

*Why we say, "Bless you!" In the Middle Ages, when influenza epidemics wiped out hundreds of thousands in a couple of weeks, a sneeze was usually the first sign the victim had been bitten by the fatal bug. The doomed person's friends would mutter "God bless you" and scurry off as fast as their feet would carry them.

*How did colonial housewives keep their furniture and floors spic-and-span without today's waxes and soaps?

They simply spat on the floor and rubbed hard with stick brushes and reed brooms. That's where we get "spit and polish."

*Michelangelo believed in glorifying the human body, and he wasn't keen on overloading his figures with clothes. His *Last Judgment* on the walls of the Sistine Chapel caused some harsh criticism by one of the Vatican's officials because of the nudity. So Michelangelo made a few changes. He painted in the face of the clergyman and added donkey's ears and a snake's tail.

*Benjamin Franklin attended school only between the ages of eight and ten. That's all it took to produce one of the wisest and most revered men in our history.

George III called him "the most dangerous man in America."

*Thomas Nast, one of America's great political cartoonists (for *Harper's Weekly*) gave us the donkey as the Democratic Party symbol and the elephant for the Republicans.

*The first person to go over Niagara Falls in a barrel was a woman, Anna Edson Taylor. She made the journey on October 24, 1901, and escaped unhurt.

*There are more stars in the sky than there are grains of sand on all the beaches of the world. And if you don't believe it, count them.

*What are most widely reproduced and distributed paintings in history? *The Mona Lisa*? *The Last Supper*? No. The *Four Freedoms* by Norman Rockwell. Prints numbering in the tens of millions have been sent all over the world.

*The *New York Sun* paid Ella Wheeler Wilcox five dollars for her poem "Solitude," which includes the lines:

"Laugh, and the world laughs with you; Weep, and you weep alone; For the sad old earth must borrow its mirth; But has trouble enough of its own."

*In literature, the average length of a sentence is around thirty-five words. Milton sometimes has as many as three hundred in one sentence. The one sentence takes over a page of print.

*Cervantes' classic, *Don Quixote*, has been translated more than any other book except the Bible. It first appeared early in the century and was not a big hit with the upper classes. But the peasants loved it.

*Four hundred years ago, when Henry VIII was lopping off the heads of friends and foes, the victims didn't want to suffer the humiliation of being hauled through the streets of London. They preferred to go by boat down the Thames to the Tower where they entered the gloomy place through a special gate, directly from boat to prison. This gate was known then, and is known today, as the "**Watergate.**"

*Badminton originated in India, where it was known as "Poona." It was brought to England and introduced to society at the country home of the Duke of Beaufort.

Name of the estate? Badminton.

*Shakespeare, who wrote with such authority about so many things, never wandered farther from his home than the distance between Boston and New York.

*Women on average use twenty thousand words a day while men use only seven thousand.

*Women on average speak twice as fast as men do.

Humor from the FART Dictionary (Scott A. Sorenson)

Please take heart. At the home of the host after a meal, if you belch, you are saying you enjoyed the meal and if you fart, it's a "thank you" card.

Did you know Benjamin Franklin wrote a book titled" *Fart Proudly*". That makes him a "for-fart-father of the USA."

"He that is conscious of

A Stink in his Breeches, is jealous of every Wrinkle in another's Nose" Benjamin Franklin.

This book is a collector's item. I would recommend it for a spot of breezy reading.

From the FART Dictionary:

There are for your information different kinds of farts. Here's a sample.

*Abraham Lincoln fart: a fart released by the orator during an important speech.

*Air-raid fart: a fart so disgusting you need to warn others immediately.

*Bombastic fart: a fart that wasn't that great, but the farter won't stop bragging about it.

*Castro fart: a fart that smells like a bad cigar.

*Cyclone fart: a fart with such power it sucks in and destroys all surrounding farts.

*Dead-end fart: a fart you mistakenly released at the end of a hallway or corridor, and now there's no means of escape.

*Ding-dong fart: a fart you let go before answering the front door to save yourself the embarrassment of farting in front of company.

*Dinner-guest fart: you thought you left your fart in the bathroom, but no, it followed you all the way to the dining table.

*El Niño fart: an unusually warm fart that drifts across the pool.

*Exit-backwards fart: a fart that leads you to leave the room without turning around for fear of what others may see on the backside of your pants.

*Fly-swatter fart: a fart in public that earns you a slap on the butt from mom.

*Hangover fart: a fart that causes the whole room to spin.

*Javelin fart: an outdoor fart with distance capability.

*Hesitant fart: a fart cautiously let go a bit at a time for fear of attachments.

*Kardashian fart: a fart you can't keep up with.

*Lapdog fart: a fart let go with a dog in your lap, which completely exonerates you from any suspicion.

*MIA fart: you know you farted, but now you can't find it.

*Octo fart: a fart that's precisely eight times more foul than anything you've ever smelled in your lifetime.

*Odyssey fart: a fart that lingers and drifts for what seems like an eternity.

*Quarantine fart: a fart that has to be left in the room with the door shut.

*Rabbit fart: a fart with a stench that multiplies rapidly.

*Reluctant fart: you have to fart, but if you stand and exit you risk the possibility of "walk and release," so you take your chances while sitting and let go a little at a time.

*Seven-dwarfs fart: any series of tiny farts that follow a large fart.

*Skip-dessert fart: a fart that has ruined dinner.

*Snail fart: a fart that creeps across the room at a very slow pace.

Humor in Bathroom Walls

Here I sit jokes.

*If you can piss this high, join the fire department. Men's.

*Make love, not war. Hell, do both: Get married.

*If you tinkle and you sprinkle

Be a sweetie, wipe the seatie.

*Sticks and stones may break my bones,

But whips and chains excite me,

So . . . throw me down,

And tie me up and show me that you love me."

*Here I sit I'm at a loss

Trying to shit out Taco sauce

I know I'm gonna drop a load

I only hope I don't explode.

*A kiss is two questions answered at once.

*Toilet Tennis:

Written on the left wall:

Look Right.

Written on the right wall:

Look left.

This could keep you going for a while.

*Here I sit

Broken-hearted,

Come to shit

But only farted.

*I stink therefore I am.

Humor in Spoof

A mocking imitation of someone or something, usually light and good-humored lampoon or parody—hoax or a prank. To get a flavor of what a spoof is, one must look to the motion picture genre, Mel Brook's, Blazing Saddles.

*Man: Hello.

Woman: Honey, it's me. Are you at the club?

Man: Yes.

Woman: I'm at the mall now and found this beautiful leather coat. It's only $1,000. Is it OK if I buy it?"

Man: Sure, go ahead if you like it that much.

Woman: I also stopped by the Mercedes dealership and saw the new 2012 models. I saw one I really liked.

Man: How much?

Woman: $80,000

Man: OK, but for that price I want it with all the options.

Woman: Great! Oh, and one more thing. The house we wanted last year is back on the market. They're asking $950,000.

Man: Well, then go ahead and give them an offer, but just offer $900,000.

Woman: OK. I'll see you later. I love you.

Man: Bye. I love you too.

The man hangs up. The other men in the locker room are looking at him in astonishment. Then he smiles and asks, "Anyone know whose phone is xxxxx?"

*Honey, What's for supper?"

An elderly gentleman of eighty-five years feared his wife was getting hard of hearing. So one day he called her doctor to make an appointment to have her hearing checked. The doctor made an appointment for a hearing test in two weeks, and meanwhile there's a simple informal test, the husband could do to give the doctor some idea of the state of her problem.

"Here's what you do," said the doctor. "Start out about forty feet away from her, and in a normal conversational speaking tone and see if she hears you. If not, go to thirty feet, then twenty feet, and so on until you get a response."

That evening, the wife is in the kitchen cooking dinner, and he's in the living room. He says to himself, "I'm about forty feet away, let's see what happens." Then in a normal tone he asks, "Honey, what's for supper?" No response.

So the husband moved to the other end of the room, about thirty feet from his wife and asks, "Honey, what's for supper?"

Still no response.

Next he moves into the dining room, where he is about twenty feet from his wife and asks, "Honey, what's for supper?"

Again he gets no response.

So he walks right up behind her. "Honey, what's for supper?"

"Damn it, Earl, for the fifth time, *chicken*!"

*A tramp lies down and sleeps in the park. He had been sleeping for about five minutes when a couple walked by. The man stopped, woke the tramp up, and asked him, "Excuse me. Do you know what the time is?" The tramp replied, "I'm sorry—I don't have a watch, so I don't know the time."

The man apologized for waking the tramp and the couple walked away.

The tramp lay down again, and after a few minutes went back to sleep. Just then, a woman, who was out walking a dog, shook the tramp's shoulder until he woke up again.

The woman said, "I'm sorry to trouble you, but I'm afraid I've lost my watch. Do you happen to know the time?" The tramp was little annoyed at being woken again, but he politely told the woman that he didn't have a watch and didn't know the time.

After the woman had gone, the tramp had an idea.

He opened the bag that contained all his possessions and got out a pen, a piece of paper, and some string. On the paper, he wrote down, "I do not have a watch. I do not know the time." He then hung the paper round his neck and eventually dropped off again.

After about fifteen minutes, a policeman who was walking through the park noticed the tramp asleep on the bench, and the sign round his neck.

He woke the tramp up and said, "I read your sign. I thought you'd like to know that it's 2:30 p.m."

*Early one morning, a mother went in to wake up her son. "Wake up, Son. It's time to go to school."

"Why, Mom, I don't want to go."

"Give me two reasons why you don't want to go."

"Well, the kids hate me for one, and the teachers hate me too."

"Oh, that's no reason not to go to school. Come on now and get ready."

"Give me two reasons why I should go to school."

"Well, for one, you're fifty-two years old. And for another, you're the Principal."

Humor in Political Correctness

The term connotes language, ideas, and behavior unconstrained by a perceived orthodoxy or by concerns about offending or expressing bias regarding various groups of people.

We do not sometimes realize that we are hurting people by using 'hurtful' words. It is therefore safe and makes good sense to be politically correct. The following excerpt from S.I. Hiyakawa's "Language in thought and action" illustrates this point.

"A distinguished negro sociologist tells of an incident in his adolescence when he was hitchhiking far from home in regions where Negroes are hardly ever seen. He was befriended by an extremely kindly white couple who

fed him and gave him a place to sleep in their home. However, they kept calling him "little nigger"—a fact which upset him profoundly even while he was grateful for their kindness. He finally got up courage to ask the man not to call him by that "insulting term."

"Who's insultin' you, son?" said the man.

"You are, sir—that name you're always calling me."

"What name?"

"Uh . . . you know."

"I ain't callin' you no names, son."

"I mean your calling me "nigger."

"Well, what's insultin' about that? You are a nigger, ain't you?"

Don't say:	Say
Black, Negro:	*African American.*
Merry Christmas:	*Happy Holidays.*
Bald:	*Comb-free.*
Body odor:	*Nondiscretionary fragrance.*
Broken home:	*Dysfunctional family.*
Bum:	*Displaced homeowner.*
Corpse:	*Terminally inconvenienced.*
Fat:	*Person of substance.*
Garbage man:	*Sanitation engineer.*

Large nose:	*Nasally gifted.*
Mercy killing:	*Euthanasia.*
Dwarf, little people:	*Vertically challenged.*
Mute, dumb:	*Verbally challenged.*
Plagiarism:	*Previously owned prose.*
Poor:	*Economically marginalized.*
Postman:	*Letter carrier.*
Prisoner:	*Client of the correctional system.*
Prostitute:	*Sex care provider.*
Really big nosed:	*Nasally disadvantaged.*
Refugees:	*Asylum seekers.*
Shoplifter:	*Cost-of-living adjustment specialist.*
Slum:	*Economic oppression zone.*
Stupid:	*Intellectually impaired.*
Too tall:	*People of height.*
Unemployed:	*Involuntarily leisured.*
Her breasts sag.	*Her breasts have lost their vertical hold.*
She does not have a great butt:	*She is gluteus to the maximus.*
She is a bad cook:	*She is microwave compatible.*

She is not a gossip:	*She is a verbal terminator.*
He gets lost all the time:	*He discovers alternate destinations.*
He farts and belches:	*He is gastronomically expressive.*
A student is lazy:	*He's energetically declined.*
You're not sleeping in class:	*You're rationing consciousness.*
You're not late:	*You just have rescheduled arrival time.*
Haves and have-nots:	*Haves and soon-to-haves.*

*Waiter: Would you have coffee, sir?

Customer: Yes. Black coffee please.

Waiter: Excuse me, sir. That's uncalled for. It's coffee without milk.

Customer: You, liberal xxx.

Humor in Signs

*Sign in doctor's office: Doctor is very busy. Please have your symptoms ready.

*Sign in coffee shop: Do not insult our waitresses by tipping them.

*Sign on each table in the same coffee shop, on a card box with a slit across the top: "Insults."

*Sign on a truck carrying explosives: Give me room or we both go boom!

*Sign in the window of a Washington, DC laundry: We do not tear your clothes with machinery. We do it carefully by hand.

*Sign in the rear of a school bus in Erie, Pennsylvania: Approach with care: Driver under the influence of children.

*Sign in a Denver motel: Do not smoke in bed without umbrella; Extra-sensitive sprinkler system.

*Sign on a plumbing truck in Elko, Nevada: Sewers drained, pipes unplugged, and if there's anything your husband has fixed lately, I can repair that too.

*Sign in a beauty shoppe in Tampa, Florida: We can give you the new look if you still have the old parts.

*Sign on a hot dog stand near the bus garage in West Hollywood, California: Bus drivers must have exact change.

*Sign on a university bulletin board: Shoes are required to eat in the cafeteria.

*Sign attached to the same sign. Socks can eat wherever they want to.

*Sign in a dinner theater in New Jersey: Do not photograph the performers while they are on stage. You may come back stage and shoot them after the show.

*Sign on a country road in Arkansas: When this sign is under water, road is impassable.

*Use stairs for rest room.

*All of the water served here has been personally passed by the manager.

*Sign in a zoo in Washington: Lost children will be taken to the Lion House. The lions are fed at 3:00 p.m.

*In a barber salon: "Curl up n' dye.

*At a lumber yard: Come see, come saw.

*At the tire store: We skid you not.

At the children's park in Wilmette: Play it safe.

On the tips jar in the Golden Gate park, San Francisco: For good karma.

*On trash can: Keep litter in its place.

* In Hamden. "Books & Company"

Humor in Toasting and Hoisting

A toast is a ritual in which a drink is taken as an expression of honor or goodwill. A toast can be sentimental, cynical, lyric, comic, defiant, long, short, or even just a single word. Toasting is a very old custom. For anyone who will ever face a sea of expectantly raised glasses. Ulysses drank to the health of Achilles in Odyssey.

We must ensure that it does not end up thus: In 1975, President Kenneth Kaunda of Zambia startled the guests at a White House dinner when he responded to a traditional toast from President Gerald Ford with a twenty-minute "toast" which was in fact a statement of his nation's foreign policy.

*Here's to the bride

And here's to the groom

And to the bride's father

Who'll pay for this room.

*I drink to your health when I'm with you,

I drink to your health when I'm alone,

I drink to your health so often,

I'm starting to worry about my own.

*When we drink, we get drunk.

When we get drunk we fall asleep.

When we fall asleep, we commit no sin.

When we commit no sin, we go to heaven.

*Here's to our hostess considerate and sweet;

Her wit is endless, but when do we eat?

*He who goes to bed, and goes to bed sober,

Falls as the leaves do, and dies in October;

But he who goes to bed, and does so mellow,

Lives as he ought to, and dies a good fellow.

*The groom and the bride get the thrill

And the guests get a drink and their fill.

But as you dance by

You will hear a big sigh

From her father who picked up the bill!

*Here's to being single

Drinking doubles

And seeing triple!

*I'll drink to the girls who do!

I'll drink to the girls who don't!

Bu I won't drink to girls

Who say they will and won't.

Humor in Jingles

A jingle is a short tune used in advertising and for other commercial uses.

A Turkey's Prayer

*I'm a little turkey to say.

Try some beef on *Thanksgiving Day.*

Turkey is tough and turkey is dry.

You really should give chicken a try!

Or how 'bout a plate of veggie delight

For a Thanksgiving dinner that tastes just right?

Dinner Bells Dashing through our food,

With a knife and fork so fast,

Corn and peas to go,

While through the throat they pass,

Into the tummy they plop,

Making growling stop,

So, oh what fun it is to eat

And eat until we drop!

Oh, dinner bells, shotgun shells.

Turkey got away

What are we supposed to do?

On our Thanksgiving Day?

A sledding we will go

(A hunting we will go)

A sledding we will go

A sledding we will go

We'll hold on tight and sit just right

And down the hill we'll go

Wheeeeeeeeee!

(Sung to "Jingle Bells")

The Pilgrims Came

The pilgrims came across the sea,

And never thought of you and me

And yet, it's very strange the way

We think of them on Thanksgiving Day.

We tell their story old and true,

Of how they sailed across the blue.

And found a new land to be free,

And built their homes quite near the sea.

Every child knows well the tale

Of how they bravely turned the sail,

And journeyed many a day and night

To worship God as they thought right.

(Sung to "Yankee Doodle")

Humor in Clichés

A cliché is an expression, idea, or element of an artistic work which has been overused to the point of losing its original meaning or effect, especially when at some earlier time it was considered meaningful or novel.

*You can only milk a dead cow once.

*A hair in the head is worth six on the back.

*You can't trade shoes with a barefoot monkey.

*There are two sides to every waffle. (*That's a Romney.*)

*You can't fill a hat with maybes.

*A pit in a peach is worth six in a bucket.

*It only rains blood in Idaho.

*An honest man eats soap.

*There's never enough time to chew all the ice.

*A paper clip won't make the dog sit up.

*Nobody is too tall for pudding.

*A potato with no eyes is better than a calendar with no days.

*Anybody can be on top if they take the elevator.

*A stapler to the head is the strongest motivator.

*He folded like a wet watermelon.

*You're looking at seven, but you're eating six.

*It feels like we're walking toward Cleveland with this one.

*If you read the title, you read the index.

*Every pig gets twisted some weeks.

*I haven't seen you in a year of sunshines.

*You can't bend steel with tears.

*It's worth all you've got plus five pizzas.

*First one shaved means last one buried.

*It's the last pair of pants that'll get ya!

*As far as I'm concerned, she hangs the moon and neatly folds the sun.

*This guy's the proverbial doctor of Twistin'!

*Happiness is the result of careful editing.

*Failure runs in the family.

*It's like they always say, list comedy is the last resort of the incompetent hack.

(Source: capnwacky.com)

Humor in Answering Machine Jingles

Jingle Bells

Jingle bells, jingle bells
Goes my phone all day
And I really want to hear
Just what you have to say.
You rang up; don't hang up
Listen for the tone
Tell me what you called me for
And I'll be sure to phone.

God Rest Ye Merry Gentlemen

I know you hate these darn machines
And I just made things worse
But if you leave your message now
I won't sing every verse.
But wait until you hear the beep
Then you know what to do
And I promise
I'll get back to you
. . . soon as I can
Yes, I pro-mise
So what more can I do?

We wish you a Merry Christmas

I wish you a Merry Christmas

I'm sorry I had to miss this

But please leave a cheery message

And I'll call you right back!

Hark the Herald Angels Sing

Hark the herald phone doth ring

Sorry I'm just here to sing

Phone recorders drive us wild

So we must be reconciled

Don't go jumping off the deep end

Leave a message at the beep end

I will listen to it all

Then you can count on me to call.

Joy to the World

Joy to the world, your call has come

Alas, but I'm not home.

So if you're selling auto glass,

Investment funds, or greener grass,

My carpets cleaned for free,

Or another charity,

Leave your number, but for your sake

Don't hold your breath.

Anyone else, leave a message at the beep.

Deck the Halls

I check my calls unless I'm stalling

Fa la, la, la, la, la, la, la

At the beep just say who's calling

Fa la, la, la, la, la, la, la.

Little Town of Bethlehem

I'll just be gone a little while

And when I return I'll phone

So leave your message with a smile

As soon as you hear the tone.

We Three Kings

Listeners are not very far

In the tub or off in a car

But I need to know who's calling

So let me know who you are.

Oh-Oh.

At the beep just say your thing

Shortly I'll give you a ring

This proceeding must be leading

To another ring-a-ling.

Away in a Manger

We're away at the moment

Your welcome call came

Your call is important

So please leave your name

The beep will alert you

You're on the right track

We'll never desert you

And will call you right back.

Oh Come All Ye Faithful

Oh come, don't be spiteful

Even though it'd be frightful

Hearing recorded voices seems sort of mean

Wait for the beep tho'

Tell me what you want to know

I know recorders gall you

At least they don't enthrall you

But I will surely call you

On your machine.

Good King Wenceslaus

Sorry I'm not here for you

Has to be a reason

But we've all got things to do

In this busy season.

If your message will not keep

Get your thoughts in order

When you hear the little beep

Talk to my recorder.

Humor in Wise Saws (Made to Look Otherwise)

Saw is a trite popular saying or proverb (figurative and colloquial).

*A penny saved is a penny to squander.

*A man is known by the company that he organizes.

*A bad workman quarrels with the man who calls him that.

*A bird in the hand is worth what it will bring.

*Better late than before anybody has invited you.

*Example is better than following it.

*Think twice before you speak to a friend in need.

*What is worth doing is worth the trouble of asking somebody to do it.

*Least said is soonest disavowed.

*He laughs best who laughs least.

*Speak of the devil and he will hear about it.

*Of two evils choose to be the least.

*Strike while your employer has a big contract.

*Where there's a will there's a won't.

Humor in Wit of the Staircase (After Wit)

The perfect witty response you think up after the conversation or argument has ended.

What happened: One day, while I was in the tenth grade, I went up to the history teacher's desk to ask a question about some stuff we were studying. Well, when I was bending over to point to something in the book, I started hearing these sniggers from my classmates and realized that a button on my blouse had come undone, giving the male teacher a full view of my department store-bra and tiny high school breasts. The teacher was real shy and bookish, maybe even gay, but that didn't stop the catcalls, "Show them things, baby," "Show-off slut," etc.

What I said: You don't really think I could speak? I turned super red and walked to my desk. If I would have had a self-destruct button, I would have pushed it. I would have disappeared myself. It was awful. I was mortified.

What I should have said: "Oh, shut up already and grow up, everybody. You're making a mountain out of a molehill."

The Children Were More Mature Than Him

What happened: I work at Chuck E. Cheese, and this guy came in during one of the busiest times he could be there. He is waiting in line, and I run up from the back to help the other cashiers. I say, "I can help you here, sir." He begins to go off on me about how long the lines are and how long it took me to come up and help. He is using the foulest language I had ever heard in there. I was trying to help him and trying to keep everything moving while apologizing profusely. Finally he flipped me off and took his tray.

What I said: "Have a magical day."

What I should have said: I am sorry, but is your mommy here? We can't have four-year-olds in here by themselves.

How Badly I Wanted Him

What happened: I had been absolutely crazy about this boy for over a year. I was completely obsessed. He was all I ever thought about, all I ever talked about, and I ran around telling people I was in love. He hardly knew I existed. I mean, I sat next to him every day in band, but we never talked. And apparently someone told him that I liked him. At a school dance, I finally plucked up courage to ask him to slow dance. As we were dancing, he said, "Is it all right if we were . . . just friends?"

What I said: "Of course!" and then mumbled some stuff about the situation . . .

What I should have said: "What if I said no? What would you do then?"

Who's Looking?

What happened: I work as a secretary at a design firm. One day after work, I headed to the local mall to shop for a gift for my sister-in-law's birthday. It had been a long day, and I'm sure I didn't look my best in my wrinkled work clothes and flat hair. As I passed one of those cell phones kiosks, the typical cell phone salesman—you know the type, still wishes he were in high school—makes eye contact with me and says in a very matter-of-fact way, "Hey, there's this new invention called makeup. Ever heard of it? You should try it sometime."

What I said: Nothing, unfortunately. I just ignored him and kept walking.

What I should have said: "Ever heard of common decency? You should give it a try. Anyway, I'm at the mall. Who am I trying to impress?"

Talking about Practice

What happened: In the corner of my teachers classroom was one of those large Fisher Price basketball hoops. I was sitting right in front of it during one class. Just as class quieted down, I shot the ball over my head but missed. Everyone is looking, and a girl on the other side of the room says, "Nice shot, Iverson."

What I said: I blushed, said nothing, and smiled.

What I should have said: "Thanks, Mutombo."

The Dentist

What happened: I went to the dentist a few years back, and once I was stretched out on the "dental couch" with a yard of equipment in my mouth, my dentist asked me, "Why is it that all dancers have small breasts?" I'm sure I was beet red as I was a former dancer.

What I said: I couldn't say much of anything.

What I should have said: "For the same reason that all dentists have small drills."

Six Feet Under

What happened: A while back, I fell madly in love with a girl who I thought was perfect. But after we started to get a little more intimate, she started asking weird questions . . . One day she asked me what would I do if she ever died . . .

What I said: "Well, I dunno . . . I would be sad and heartbroken."

What I should have said: "Well, why don't you die and we find out . . ."

It's for You

What happened: This was in school years ago. We weren't allowed to wear jewelry. Everyone tried to sneak a little of it on—just the way kids want to appear clever . . . Most of the teachers didn't care, but some of them took it really seriously. Standing in line one day, a particular old bat jetted over and shouted "Ring."

What I said: Took it off mumbling and handed it over.

What I should have said: "Hello."

It's Not You . . . It's Your Mom

What happened: A few years ago, my boyfriend at the time was at a house. As we waited for the realtor, he and his mom were having a heated discussion in Spanish (which I do not understand). He finally got fed up and shouted (in English), "Ask her yourself!" So his mother turned to me and asked, "Are all the women in your family as overweight as you?"

What I said: "Ummm . . ."

What I should have said: "Are all the women in your family so rude?" Or "Have all the women in your family had as much plastic surgery as you?"

Return Trip

What happened: I'm about 5'10" with a beard, moustache, and brown hair down to about my waist. My girlfriend and I were walking out of a 7-Eleven on a Sunday morning about 1:00 a.m., and one of the homeless gentlemen of the city laid eyes upon me and said, "Wow, man . . . you look just like Jesus."

What I said: "OK" as I ducked into my car and pulled off.

What I should have said: "I'd be back."

Your Boyfriend Doesn't Think So . . .

What happened: There was a girl who always asked if I was gay because of my shoelaces. One day, she said really loudly, (insert my name) is a lesbian.

What I said: I just looked down and said I wasn't.

What I should have said: Your boyfriend doesn't think so.

Too Many Girlfriends

What happened: I was talking to my professor. He told me that I tied with somebody else for highest test grade in the class. When I asked, "Who?" He responded with "your girlfriend."

What I said: "Oh."

What I should have said: "Which one?"

Humor in New Teeth in Old Saws

It is a collection of well-known sayings done in the modern manner.

*Children should be seen and not *had.*

*'Tis better to have loved and *left.*

*There's no time like the *pleasant.*

*The apparel oft proclaims *the man when it's really a woman.*

*Sweet are the uses of *publicity.*

*Let the punishment fit the *rhyme.*

*Christmas comes but once a year's *enough.*

*Here comes the *bribe!*

*A stitch in time saves *embarrassment.*

*All's *bare* in love and war.

*A fool and his *honey* are soon parted.

*An army marches on its *enemy's stomach.*

*Eat, drink, and be merry *for to-morrow we diet.*

*Familiarity *breeds.*

*Faint heart ne'er *won argument with fair lady.*

*Take care of the pennies and the *income tax will take care of your dollars.*

*A rose by any other name will *cost as much.*

*A woman's place is *on the magazine cover.*

**Sneak* and ye shall find.

*He who hesitates *is run over.*

*Marry in haste and *repeat at leisure.*

**Invitation* is the sincerest flattery.

*One is never too old to *yearn.* (Wayne G. Haisley)

Humor in Anagrams

An anagram is a word or phrase made by transposing or rearranging the letters of another word or phrase. No letters can be used twice or left out.

Word or Phrase.	Anagram
Dormitory	*Dirty room.*
Evangelist	*Evil's agent.*
Slot machines	*Cash lost in 'em.*
Mother-in-law	*Woman Hitler.*
Snooze alarms	*Alas! No more Zzs.*
The earthquakes	*That queer shake.*
Animosity	*Is no amity.*
Semolina	*Is no meal.*
A decimal point	*I'm a dot in place.*
Contradiction	*Accord not in it.*

President Clinton of the USA	*To copulate, he finds interns.*
U.S.A. Gold	Douglas

Humor in Banter

Banter is teasing or joking with someone in a friendly way.

*Me: I'll be ready in a few minutes, come on over when you're ready.

Him: OK, Let me stop at the bank and I'll be right there.

Me: Oh, sweetie, I'm your girlfriend, you don't have to pay for it.

*Her: I want to dance like this forever!

Me: Don't you ever want to improve?

*Me: I would go to the end of the world for you!

Her: Yes, but would you stay there?

*Me: You remind me of the sea.

Her: Because I'm wild, romantic and exciting?

Me: No, because you make me sick.

*Guy you have a crush on walks up to you at a party—

"Want a coke or something?"

"Yeah, I'll take the something!"

He says, "You couldn't handle the something."

You respond, "Not unless you offer it . . ."

His comment next, "I'm not that kind of guy . . ." with a smile and a wink.

"Can you point me in the direction one who is?" returning the smile.

Humor in Freudian Slip

Freudian slip is a humorous statement which seems accidental but supposedly comes from some deep psychological disturbance. Basically, funny things said unintentionally owing to a slip of the tongue.

*A woman looking at your *rock* collection and upon viewing your prized rose quartz remarks—"*Nice cock* . . . I . . . I mean *rock*."

*For seven and a half years I've worked alongside President Reagan. We've had triumphs; made some mistakes. We've had some *sex* . . . uh . . . setbacks. (President H. W. Bush)

*Last night, I was watching "*Some Like it Hot*" with Marilyn Monroe. I was watching this scene where she was wearing a low cut dress, and my fiancé came in and watched it too. When it was over, he turned to me and said, "Ready to go to *boobs* . . . oh I mean bed?"

*President Bush in a speech he was giving a group of teachers, "I'd like to *spank* all teachers." He meant *thank* all teachers.

*We cannot let terrorists and rogue nations hold this nation *hostile* or our allies *hostile*." He meant *hostage*. (President George W. Bush)

Humor in Conundrum

A conundrum is like a riddle in that it is a word puzzle; the only problem being that while you may be able to solve a riddle, the answer to a conundrum is impossible to solve.

*If a turtle loses its shell, is it naked or homeless?

*If a black box flight recorder is never damaged in a plane crash, why don't engineers design and make the whole plane out of that stuff?

*Why are psychics still working if they know the winning lottery numbers?

*If you try to fail, but you succeed, which have you done?

*If nothing sticks to Teflon, then how do they make Teflon stick to the pan?

Humor in Catch Tale

It's basically a funny story that messes up the reader or listener by implying an awful ending and then stopping with an abrupt declaration.

*"You're a liar!" shouted the little man. "What!" roared the big man, clenching a huge fist. "Do you dare call me that, you pint-sized, hammered-down sawed-off runt?" "I do" came back the defiant reply. "If you insult me again, you big hunk of beef, you'd better watch out, or I'll cut you short!" "Cut me short, you abbreviated piece of nothing!" cried the enraged giant. "Yes, and here goes!" snapped the little man sharply. And quick as lightning, before the big fellow could utter a word, he hung up on him.

Extract from Patients' Medical Records

*Patient referred to hospital by private physician with green stools.

*Patient urinates around the clock every two hours.

*Rx: Mycostatin vaginal suppositories. Insert daily until exhausted.

Extract from Actual Church Bulletin Bloopers

"The One whose throne is in heaven sits laughing . . ." (Ps. 2: 4)

*Don't let today's pace and stress kill you. Let the church help.

*At this evening's service the sermon topic will be, "What is hell?" Come early and listen to the choir practice.

*Remember in prayer the many who are sick of our church and community.

*For those of you who have children and don't know it, we have a nursery downstairs.

*The rosebud on the altar this morning is to announce the birth of David Alan Belzer, the *sin* of Rev. and Mrs. Julius Belzer.

*Tuesday at 4:00 p.m., there will be an ice-cream social. All ladies *giving milk* will please come early.

*Pastor is on vacation. *Massages* can be given to church secretary.

*The Reverend Adams spoke *briefly* much to the *delight* of his audience.

*The preacher will preach his farewell message, after which the choir will sing, "Break Forth with Joy."

Sarcasm

It is a form of verbal irony expressing personal disapproval in the guise of praise.

In the Bible in Ecclesiastes 11: 9 reads, "Rejoice, young man, during your childhood, and let your heart be pleasant during the days of young manhood. And allow for impulses of your heart and the desires of your eyes. Yet know that God will bring you to judgment for all these things." Many biblical scholars interpret this to mean, "If you want to be judged by God, do whatever you want."

*In Exodus 14: 11, Moses, who was leading the Israelites from Egypt, was asked, "Was there a lack of graves in Egypt, that you took us away to die in the wilderness?"

*Now we know why some animals eat their own children.

*Do not let your mind wander; it's far too small to be let out on its own.

*I like you. People say I've got no taste, but I like you.

*She's the first in her family born without tail.

*That man is cruelly depriving a village somewhere of an idiot.

*Whatever it is that is eating you, it must be suffering horribly.

*You have an inferiority complex and it is fully justified.

*You should do some soul-searching. You might just find one.

*Your mind isn't so much twisted as badly sprained.

*I think therefore we have nothing in common.

*If I agreed with you, we'd both be wrong.

*Everyone has the right to be stupid but you are abusing the privilege.

*If I got smart with you how would you know?

*If things get any worse, I'll have to ask you to stop helping me.

*I refuse to have a battle of wits with an unarmed person.

*Roses are red, violets are blue

Monkeys like you should be kept in the zoo

Don't feel so angry, you will find me there too.

Not in a cage but laughing at you.

*Twinkle, Twinkle little star

You should know what you are

And once you know what you are

Mental hospital is not so far.

*The rain makes all things beautiful

The grass and flowers too

If rain makes all things beautiful

Why doesn't it rain on you?"

*I wrote your name on sand it got washed

I wrote your name in air, it was blown away

Then I wrote your name on my heart

And I got a heart attack straight away.

Humorous Grammar

The light side of grammar.

*Verbs *have* to agree with their subjects.

*Never use a preposition to end a sentence *with*. Winston Churchill, corrected on this error once, responded to the young man who corrected him by saying, "Young man! That is the kind of impudence *up with which I will not put!*"

**And* don't start a sentence with a conjunction.

*It is wrong to ever split an infinitive.

*Avoid clichés like the plague. (*They're old hat.*)

*Also, always *avoid annoying alliteration.*

*Be *more or less specific.*

*Parenthetical remarks (*however relevant*) are (*usually*) unnecessary.

*Also too *never, ever, use repetitive redundancies endlessly over and over again.*

*No sentence fragments.

Self-referential Humor

Self-referential or self-reflexive humor is a type of comedic expression that either directed toward some other subject or openly directed toward itself.

Classic self-referential humor: This from Chief Justice William Rehnquist.

"I've often started off with a lawyer joke, complete caricature of a lawyer who's been nasty, greedy and unethical. But I've stopped that practice. I gradually realized that the *lawyers* didn't think the jokes were funny and the *non-lawyers* didn't know they were jokes."

*I'm the humblest person I know.

*I used to think I was indecisive, but now I'm not sure.

*The workshop on procrastination has been canceled, as no one got around to enrolling.

*Anyone who visits a psychiatrist ought to have his head examined.

*87.5 percent of all statistics are made up.

*I'm trying to be self-deprecating, but I really suck at it. (Eric Knibbe)

*I'd give my right hand to be ambidextrous.

*All generalizations are wrong. (Vivek Dhar)

**I thought about changing my mind, but then I reconsidered. (Brian Haynes)

Hoping these suggestions will be helpful.

Excerpts: From *Les Reflections d' Ebn Goha* by J. Ascar Nahas, Paris, 1945.

*Do not fight if you are sure to be the loser.

*Before thanking the one who offers you a jewel box, see what the box contains.

*Stay in the shadow of your leader, he will give you his light.

*One must learn to arrive when you are wanted and to leave before you are no longer wanted.

*The last word belongs to him who hollers the longest, not the loudest.

*Don't ask for mercy before knowing if you are in danger.

*When your wife is in labor, don't speak of your bellyache.

*Undertake only a few things but do them well. One judges the soldier by his victories not the number of his battles.

*Don't stir up a problem when you don't want to be faced with solving it.

*If you don't want to be shoved, don't put yourself in the way.

*Don't say that your enemy cannot conquer you if you are out of his reach. The monkey, at the top of the tree, easily mocks the elephant.

*The more you reveal, the less you are interesting. The open book attracts little notice.

*If you hold the tail of your donkey, don't complain of his kicks.

*Throw a dog a bone if you don't want him to covet your meat.

*If you cut the wings of the bird, don't ask him to fly.

*Spend half of your time mistrusting others and the other half mistrusting yourself.

Putting Humor to Work

At social gatherings, friends bandy jokes, swap yarns—where the fish that got away got bigger with each telling and the near miss on the highway gets more hair-raising with each retelling, jeers, jabs and jibes, draw the long bow, trade shaggy dog stories, with back-slapping familiarity, and having used humor as a lubrication for social inter action leave for their homes having had a good time. In this instance, humor was an end in itself. It performed brilliantly the task it was assigned—make everyone happy. This is because we have a much better claim to the title *Homo ridens* (laughing man) than to *Homo sapiens* (human being).

Humor can be used as a communication tool, as a blunderbuss, as a crutch, and sometimes just for the sheer exhilaration of it. It can be called upon to help out in various other ways and as a means to an end. If you want to tell people the truth, make them laugh. On the surface there's one thing, deeper, there is more.

Cicero used humor in public speaking. He put exaggeration, sarcasm, punning, and other techniques to work for him. Lewis Carroll in *Alice in Wonderland* teaches children and adults that the way to live in harmony in society is to get along—the same way as Alice conducted herself with all the animals in Wonderland. It's a story of personal growth. As

Alice makes her way through Wonderland, we see her grow as a person—from a frightened girl to a young woman who matures as a result of her adventures. All this is related with great deal of humor to hold the children's attention. During the horrendous time of the holocaust the Jews and during the dark antebellum years the Negro slaves embraced humor and religion—religion for a better next world and humor for emotional release in this. Humor was a survival tactic and a buffer to social injustice. Humor during time of repression was focused on what was wrong with society; it brought the oppressed together, and it helped them to cope immensely. All these body marks can be visible in the following story.

*Goebbels was touring German schools. At one, he asked the students to call out patriotic slogans.

"Hail Hitler," shouted one child.

"Very good," said Goebbels.

"Deutschland uber alles," another called out.

"Excellent! How about a stronger slogan."

A hand shot up, and Goebbels nodded.

"Our people shall live forever," the little boy said.

"Wonderful" exclaimed Goebbels. "What is your name, young man?"

"Israel Goldberg, sir."

Mark Twain said, "The secret source of humor is not joy but sorrow."

And Shelley in "To a Skylark."

"Our sincerest laughter

With some pain is fraught

Our sweetest songs are those that tell us of saddest thought."

Humor earned Nathaniel a prominent position in the Christian hierarchy. Nathaniel is told that Jesus is from Nazareth, and his mischievous reaction was "Can anything good come from Nazareth?" knowing full well that Jesus is from Nazareth. Jesus had a sense of humor. He felt that this is a guy he could trust and invited him to join the Apostles. The Gospel writers had a sense of humor and so preserved this fact for over two thousand years.

Humor as a Weapon

The Jews and slaves employed their sense of irony as a spiritual weapon. Defenseless, they turned to humor to dispel their fear and apprehension. When victims themselves laugh at their plight to preserve their own sanity, the door is left open for others. "There is a fellowship of those who bear the mark of pain," said Albert Schweitzer. For instance, the Jews in sealed rooms, during alerts, made jokes to keep their spirits from sagging. Heartily laughing together at the same thing forms an immediate bond, much as enthusiasm for the same ideal does. A "joking relationship" is formed. Humor is one of the greatest gifts God gave mankind to pull itself out of despair. Individuals with an appreciation for humor have an advantage over those who don't—that it will be easier for them to maintain community membership. Political jokes are tiny revolutions. Every political joke brings the great man down to a human (or inhuman) level; every joke deflates his bombast and megalomania; every joke gives hope and self-confidence to the oppressed. The greater the weight of repression, the bitterer will be the satire. The more excruciating the slavery, the more exquisite the buffoonery becomes.

I give below stray examples of how Jews during the holocaust and the Negroes during slavery employed humor as a weapon to stay sane.

From the 1855 slave narrative *From Slave Cabin to Pulpit* by Peter Randolph.

*Pompey and the Jackass

Master: Pompey, how do I look? (The master asked.)

Slave: O, massa mighty. You looks mighty.

Master: What do you mean "mighty," Pompey?

Slave: Why, massa, you looks noble.

Master: What do you mean by "noble"?

Slave: Why, suh, you looks just like a lion.

Master: Why, Pompey, where have you seen a lion?

Slave: I saw one down in yonder field the other day, massa.

Master: Pompey, you foolish fellow, that was a jackass.

Slave: Was it, massa? Well, suh, you looks just like him.

*Master: "You scoundrel, you ate my turkey." (A master scolds a young slave.)

Slave: "Yes, suh, massa, you got less turkey but you suh got more nigger."

*Jews when being carried away to the concentration camp would ask one another, "Do you believe in life after wagon?"

*Two Jews in Berlin are discussing their plight.

"Terrible," says one, "persecutions, no rations, discriminations and quotas. Sometimes I think we would have been better off if we had never been born."

"Sure," says his friend, "but who has that much luck—may be one in fifty thousand."

*Two Jews meet in Warsaw, and one of them is eating a perfumed soap. The other asks, "Moyshe, why are you eating soap with such a scent?"

He answers, "If they turn me into soap, I might as well smell nice."

*Czechoslovakians during the Nazi occupation began surreptitiously painting walls with jokes directed at the occupiers. Despite their attempts to erase the graffiti and suppress the practice, the Nazis were demoralized while the Czechs experienced a significant boost in morale. This is employment of humor in its truest form.

Much has been written about how humor can be put to good use. Prominent writers have devoted a whole book to this subject. This chapter is to give you a feel of the potential that is in humor.

Speaking Truth to Power through Humor

Presidents and prime ministers in modern democracies like autocratic kings in times gone by tend to live in a "cocoon," cut off from the hoi polloi surrounded by sycophants. In order to be effective rulers, they yearn to learn what people on the streets thought of their rule. In a democracy, presidents and prime ministers get an earful from polls and a free media. Kings in the past sometimes traveled the land incognito and learned for themselves. They also employed jesters or clowns also known as "fool" to tell them what ails the people. The fool did so by couching his scathing comments in humor. He was expected to hold up the mirror to kings and queens so that they may see their flaws. Queen Elizabeth went so far as to rebuke a fool called Clod for not criticizing her.

*A jester called Claus Narr was employed by the Elector of Saxony. His master at this time could not beget an heir. He let his boss know how this could be solved. "You should study the methods of the monks," said Claus, "they have no wives, but they manage to have plenty of children, so no doubt they grow them in their gardens."

The fool, the clown, or the court jester of medieval times was employed not only for his juggling skills, but also for his judgment, perception, inventive thought, and wisdom which was highly valued.

*In 1386, the Duke of Austria, Leopold the Pious, asked his jester for his opinion on his plans to attack the Swiss. His jester, Jenny von Stockach, espousing the "Powell Doctrine" bluntly said, "You fools, you're all debating how to get into the country, but none of you have thought how you're going to get out again." The king failed to listen, and the army suffered badly.

In Shakespeare's *Twelfth Night* we see the Fool's proximity to power.

Feste: Good Madonna, why mourn'st thou?

Olivia: Good fool, for my brother's death.

Feste: I think his soul is in hell, Madonna.

Olivia: I know his soul is in heaven, fool.

And Feste the fool lets her have it. "The more fool, Madonna, to mourn for your brother's soul, being in heaven."

Fools were the voice of reason to Kings and Princes. This, in King Lear: Lear allows the Fool to be openly critical of him, while requiring absolute obedience and flattery from everyone else.

Lear: Dost thou call me Fool, Boy?

Fool: "All thy other titles thou hast given away; that, thou was born with." Stated simply the Fool is telling the King you were born a fool.

Humor to Ease Tension in Serious Literature

Fiction and Non Fiction are just two different ways of lying to try to get at the *truths*. Fiction lies by fabricating what isn't there. Non Fiction lies by omitting what is. (Moshin Hamid reviewing Nell Freudenberger's novel *The Newlyweds*)

"Novelists and playwrights have employed humor in serious works with a view to easing tension providing a kind of comic relief. In the Iliad, that dignified epic story of the Trojan War, scenes of bloody combat are regularly relieved by mirthful antics of gods and goddesses on Mount Olympus. What is perhaps the most poignant scene in the Iliad, Hector's farewell to his wife Andromache and child is carefully interwoven with humor." Author A. Rapp says it constitutes a classic of the *Laughter and Tears* class.

In *A Tale of Two Cities.*

Charles Dickens's *A Tale of Two Cities* is a serious work of fiction with the French Revolution as its backdrop with its attendant killings and chaos. Dickens writes, "Whenever any reference (however slight) is made here to the condition of the French people before or during the revolution, it is truly made on the faith of the most trustworthy witness. It has been one of my hopes," he writes, "to add something to the popular and picturesque means of understanding *that terrible time.*"

A story of love, this story tells us the extent to which a person will go to demonstrate his love. Sydney Carton loved Lucie Manette, but he did not have a "ghost of a chance," for she was in love with Charles Darnay. Darnay is arrested for being an aristocrat and was destined for the guillotine; Carton resembled Darnay very closely. He tricks Darnay into trading places with him and is killed. Sydney Carton an alcoholic makes peace with himself, "It is a far, far better thing that I do, than I have ever done; it is a far, far better rest that I go to than I have ever known." Charles Dickens begins this serious novel thus:

There was a king with a large jaw and a queen with a plain face on the throne of England; there was a king with a large jaw and a queen with a fair face, on the throne of France.

In Ayn Rand's *Fountainhead*

Howard Roark the protagonist of the novel is an uncompromising architect. He does what he wants as he moves through the world full of obstacles. As an orphan, he gets into a reputable architecture school on his own merits. He believed that you either have integrity or you don't. He refuses to conform or compromise his aesthetic integrity. Howard Roark had a profound dedication to values, to the highest and best, to the ideal. He designs really cool buildings, the likes of which nobody has ever seen and refuses to do his assignments and so the school kicks him out.

How does he face this monstrous calamity?

"Howard Roark laughed." This is how Ayn Rand begins her book. "He stood naked at the edge of a cliff. The lake lay far below him." Howard Roark laughed. We need laughter for relief of pain for, as Nietzsche says, "Man alone suffers so excruciatingly that he was compelled to invent laughter," and Byron says, "And if I laugh at any mortal thing, Tis that I may not weep." The fact is that laughter can just as well be the expression of or at least a release from grief as *joy*.

Titus Andronicus, after his daughter has been ravished, had her hands cut off, and he himself, being deprived of a hand, laughs. Marcus admonishes him, "Why dost thou laugh? It fits not with this hour!" And Titus Andronicus replies, "Why, I have not another tear to shed." When you have exhausted your stock of tears, you are left with only laughter.

Ted Cohen cites a passage from the Talmud in which a debate among scholars as to whether a cooking oven of a particular kind is ritually clean is settled on the basis not of a heavenly voice but on the principle that the majority rules. What did God say in response to this? According to the prophet Elijah, who was there when God got wind of it, he laughed saying, "My sons have defeated Me. My sons have defeated Me." God laughs thus becoming human.

In *Hamlet*: A Tragedy with Multiple Deaths

Hamlet here exacts revenge on his uncle Claudius for the murder of his father which sets off more killings.

Ophelia loved Hamlet, and his cooling affection for Ophelia drives her to her death. Hamlet is unaware that the grave is being dug to bury Ophelia. We witness a lot of humorous wordplay right in the maw of a tragedy.

Hamlet addresses the grave digger: Whose grave's this, Sirrah?

Grave digger: Mine, sir; O, a pit of clay for to be made; for such a guest is meet.

Hamlet: I think it be thine indeed, for thou liest in it.

Grave digger: You lie out on it, sir, and therefore 'tis not yours. For my part, I do not lie in it, yet it is mine.

Hamlet: Thou dost lie in it, to be in it and say it is thine. "Tis for the dead, not for the quick therefor thou liest."

Grave digger: 'Tis a quick lie, sir. 'Twill away again from me to you.

Hamlet: What man doest thou dig for?

Grave digger: For no man sir.

Hamlet: What woman, then?

Grave digger: For none, neither.

Hamlet: Who is to be buried in it?

Grave digger: One, that was a woman, sir, but, rest her soul, she's dead.

In *Macbeth*

This is another of Shakespeare's tragedies. It's about a regicide and its tragic aftermath. Macbeth kills King Duncan on the urgings of his ambitious, wily wife and tragedy follows. Shakespeare makes room for some fun.

Macduff: Was it so late, friend, ere you gone to bed; that you do lie so late?

Porter: Faith, sir, we were carousing till the second cock; and drink, sir, is a great provoker of three things.

Macduff: What three things does drink especially provoke?

Porter: Marry, sir, nose-painting, sleep, and urine. Lechery, sir, provokes, and unprovokes: it provokes the desire, but it takes away the performance.

Humor to Expose Society's Shortcomings

*In *A Tale of Two Cities*, Charles Dickens draws the reader's attention to spousal abuse. Jerry Cruncher is totally unjustified yelling at his wife. Cruncher even accuses his wife of praying against him.

"What!" said Mr. Cruncher, looking out of bed for a boot? "You're at it agin, are you?"

"I was only saying my prayers."

"Saying your prayers? You're a nice woman! What do you mean by flopping yourself down and praying agin me?"

*Dickens pokes fun of the conditions of banks during his time.

"Cramped in all kinds of dim cupboards and hutches at Tellson's, the oldest men carried on the business gravely. When they took a young man into Tellson's London house, they hid him somewhere till he was old. They kept him in a dark place, like a cheese, until he had the full Tellson flavor and blue—mold upon him."

*Shakespeare in all his comedies managed to express a concern about the unequal treatment of the sexes. In *Taming of the Shrew*, he portrayed with harshness the injustice done to women in fashionable society.

Taming of the Shrew on one level is a comedy that provokes laughter. Beneath it all, we see the shabby treatment of Katherina by Petruchio. As Cicero put it "An indecency decently put is the thing we laugh hardest." By physical and verbal abuse Petruchio domesticates an ebullient, pretty and witty Katherina. To an extent she becomes humiliatingly servile, willing to say or do anything not to incur Petruchio's wrath.

In this exchange between Petruchio and Katherina, we see Petruchio's total dominance over Katherina.

Petruchio: Come on, a God's name; once more toward our fathers.

Good Lord, how bright and goodly shines the moon!

Katherina: The moon! The sun: it is not moonlight now.

Petruchio: I say it is the moon that shines so bright.

Katherina: I know it is the sun that shines so bright.

Petruchio: Now, by my mother's son, that's my-self, it shall be moon or star or what I list . . .

Hortensio: Say as he says or we shall never go.

Katherina: Forward, I pray, since we have come so far; and be it moon or sun or what you please.

And if you please to call it a rush-candle; henceforth I vow it shall be so for me.

Petruchio: I say it is the moon.

Katherina: I know it is the moon.

Petruchio: Nay, then you lie; it is the blessed sun.

Katherina: Then God be blessed, it is the blessed sun! But sun it is not when you say it is not;

And the moon changes even as your mind; what you will have it named, even that it is; and it shall be so for Katherine.

By introducing humor authors attract readers to their books and are able to convey their message in a less didactic tone. By making it humorous, authors help the reader retain the message.

*In the *Dialogue of the Dogs*," Cervantes gives the gift of speech for a day to two dogs—Berganza and the critical Scipio. They set about satirizing humans—the butcher, constable, and merchant, exposing their corrupt ways. It is comical and yet he drives home the moral with telling effect.

A philandering husband, who given syphilis by his wife, is hospitalized. One feverish night, he overhears the hospital guard dogs telling each other their life's story—a wickedly ironic tale where the virtuous canines find themselves victim, time and time again, to deceitful humans. As Berganza tells Scipio about the different masters he has had over the years, he simultaneously transmits Cervantes' commentary on the vagaries of human nature.

Berganza tells his life by describing the series of masters he has had throughout his life. Through Berganza's tale, the reader is privy to the vices that can be seen in the political and social sphere. By means of the conversation between Berganza and Scipio, Cervantes also draws comic attention to the spiritual ignorance of the common man and the emptiness of religious observance.

Berganza: "Nothing surprised me so much, or seemed worse to me, than to see how those butchers (in the slaughter house) kill a man as readily as a cow."

Scipio tells Berganza: "Gossip is not a good thing if it kills one person, even though it makes many laugh. And if you can please without it, I shall consider you very wise."

"The lords of the earth are very different from Him of heaven. The former, before they hire a servant, first investigate his origin, test his ability, take note of his appearance, and even want to know what clothes he owns. But to enter the service of God, the poorest is the richest, the lowliest, of highest lineage, if only he has a clean heart and the wish to serve

Him, he is at once entered on the pay-roll, and his wages are so good that in abundance and amount they almost exceed his desire."

And Berganza: "Humility is the foundation and corner stone of all virtues, and without it none of the others exist. Oh, friend Scipio, if you only knew how trying it is to pass from a state of happiness to one of infelicity! Listen: when misery and misfortunes are of long and continuous duration, or come to a quick end through death, or their persistence develops the habit and custom of suffering them, however bad, one can endure them. But when from a distressful and calamitous state, without thinking or expecting it, one passes to another of well-being, contentment, and happiness, and then, after a little while, returns to that first state and the earlier trials and misadventures, the suffering is so keen that it does not put an end to life it makes the torment of living worse than death."

Ironically Cervantes uses dogs to teach man how he should conduct himself.

At one point, Scipio tells Berganza to "shut up and proceed with your story." and, Beeganza quips, "How am I supposed to proceed if I must shut up."

Humor as a Commentary of a Social System

George Orwell's *Animal Farm* is a classic satire of the Russian Revolution—the ceaseless arrests, censored newspapers, and prowling hordes of armed police. Here is the account of the bold struggle initiated by the animals that transforms Mr. Jones's farm into a democratic animals' farm wherein all are equal. The climax as to be expected comes when bloodshed follows with the reestablishment of totalitarian rule ending in the realization that as in real life with humans. "Some animals are more equal than others." It was George

Orwell's attempt to jolt the left out of its infatuation with the Soviet Union, to strip aside the romanticization of communism and lay bare its awful reality. As such, the pigs serve as stand-ins for the Soviet leadership (as well as its precursors). Old Major, a purebred and something of a philosopher, is the Karl Marx figure laying out a vision of revolution but leaving the details of implementation to others, not to mention dying before the real action starts; Napoleon is the ruthless Stalin, cloaking totalitarianism in the language of the revered Old Major; Snowball is a doomed Trotsky, peddling an arguably less corrupt vision of animal revolt and self-rule.

On one level, children can enjoy reading the way animals conspire against Mr. Jones the owner. The serious reader will be moved by the depth of meaning in for instance these words uttered by Old Major, the pig.

"Man is the only creature that consumes without producing. He does not give milk, he does not lay eggs, he's too weak to pull the plough, cannot run fast enough to catch rabbits. Yet he is lord of all animals. He sets them to work, he gives back to them the bare minimum that will prevent them from starving, and the rest he keeps to himself." One observes here the ugly face of capitalism—the exploitation of the workers by the wealthy.

Having experimented democracy with animals Orwell's conclusion is "all animals are equal"—like humans—"but some animals are more equal than others."

Humor in the Darkest Times

A fine illustration of humor sustaining people through the darkest, bitterest times we find in the "The Diary of Anne Frank."

She writes freely of the laughter that resounds in their cramped attic prison in Holland. Here's a heartbreaking exchange between her and her boyfriend Peter. This is what she writes in her diary. In the midst of their privations and virtual incarceration what does Peter want from Anne?

Peter so often used to say, "Do laugh, Anne." This struck me as odd, and I asked, "Why must I always laugh?"

"Because I like it; you get such dimples in your cheeks when you laugh; how do they come actually?"

"I was born with them. I've got one in my chin, too. That's my only beauty!"

"Of course not. That's not true."

"Yes, it is. I know quite well that I'm not a beauty; I never have been and never shall be."

"I don't agree at all, I think you're pretty."

"That's not true."

"If I say so then you can take it from me it is!"

Then I naturally said the same of him.

Humor to the Rescue in a Stressful Situation

*A woman was keen to impress her clients with an elaborate dinner. She spent an entire day cooking and even hired someone to serve the meal. All went well until the main course. As they were bringing in the crown roast, the kitchen door hit the server from behind and the platter went flying across the room. The hostess froze, regained composure, then commanded, "Dear, don't just stand there. Pick up the roast, go in the kitchen, and get the other one."

*In his book *Man's Search for Meaning*, Viktor Frankl speaks of using humor to survive his imprisonment during WWII. He and another inmate would invent at least one amusing story daily to help them cope with their horrors.

*In Treblinka, where a day's food was stale bread and a cup of rotting soup, one prisoner cautions a fellow inmate against gluttony. "Hey, Moshe, Don't over eat. Think of us who have to carry you." (Elie Wiesel in *Night*)

*In 1981, when President Reagan was shot in the chest by a would-be assassin, he reportedly said to his doctors, "I hope you're all Republicans." This comment did more to relieve the strain on this nation than any of the broadcasts or news releases.

*The regional superior of the Jesuits in New York City was visiting the infirmary, where the sick and elderly priests and brothers lived. The superior was talking about how the Jesuits in the area were getting older and older. "We have so many aging Jesuits," said the superior, "that there really isn't any room for anyone else here in the infirmary."

To which an elderly Jesuit shouted out, "Father, we're dying as fast as we can."

Emergency medical technicians (EMTs), police officers, paramedics, and the like use humor strictly within the confines of their profession and out of earshot of the public to get through difficult days. If they do not, they will not be able to move on to the next calamity. They sorely need the release that humor and laughter provide. Laughter under these circumstances is emotionally cleansing and helps them counter the psychological gravity they experience every day on their jobs. This enables them to get on to the next assignment. Firefighters, for instance, refer to burnt bodies as crispy critters. The following examples give a flavor of their sense of humor.

*After responding to a call in which a man had committed suicide by jumping in front of a train, a member of the response team said to his buddy, "Hey, give me a hand, will ya?" (The body was dismembered.)

*After a plane crash, in which the emergency response team spent the morning putting bodies in bags, one member of the team said, "The bag lunches are here."

*Delta Air Lines suffered three crashes within a two-to-three-year period in the 1980s. Firemen and police officers were heard bandying the following jokes.

*At Delta, they now offer three classes of service—*smoking, nonsmoking, and burnt beyond recognition.*

*Delta now offers you *free drinks if you present your dental records when purchasing your ticket.*

It must be noted that these jokes may seem insensitive to people not in the field of emergency response, but they are critical in helping emergency-response officials sustain the passive frame of mind and move on to the next. Humor becomes the connecting link between tragedies.

Humor as the Politicians' Tool

*Politicians would do almost anything to be liked by voters. Humor is an ideal tool in this regard. The best-known example is President Ronald Reagan, fondly referred to as "the great communicator" and also "amiable dunce." He scored a comical bull's-eye during his first debate with Walter Mondale. There was a great disparity in their ages. Reagan was much older, and there was much speculation whether he was up to it. During the debate, he turned the tables on Mondale, remaking, "I will not hold my opponent's age against him" The audience erupted in laughter.

*President Reagan used jokes to make a point. He made it known to President Gorbachev that he is not very much liked in the Soviet Union by relating this joke to him.

Two guys are standing in line waiting for vodka. Finally, one grew impatient and says, "This is ridiculous. I'm going to go and kill Gorbachev." He leaves and comes back twenty minutes later. "Did you do it?" his friend asks him. "No," he responds. That line was even longer than this line.

*Reagan, who was endowed with practical common sense and did not put a high premium on those with book-learning, related this story to show the value of simple common sense. He said once, "I feel a little bit like the old farm gentleman who was in the bar one day," he told a crowd in

1983, "and two gentlemen with much more knowledge and sophistication than he had were discussing nuclear energy. And finally, aware of his presence and thinking, they'd have a little joke. One of them said to the old farmer, 'Where would you like to be in the event of a nuclear explosion?' and the old boy said (here is where common sense trumps academic firepower), 'Some place where I could say, *What was that?*'" The audience loved him for his humor.

*When there were problems in Panama and Congress was considering economic sanctions, Regan cracked, "If the Congress wants to bring the Panamanian economy to its knees, why doesn't it just go down there and run the country?"

*Reagan was watching some student protests with aide Lyn Nofziger during the sixties, and they spotted a long-haired guy, who seemed a bit spaced-out, waving a "Make Love, Not War" sign in the air. Reagan with characteristic humor, without malice, says, "Look at him, Lyn. He doesn't look like capable of either."

*Reagan could convey stark truth with a good laugh. A group of students once began lecturing him about how the older generation couldn't understand them. They pointedly told Regan that his generation didn't get it; they were growing up in an era with nuclear weapons, jet planes, and men shot in space. Regan put them in their place with this cutting reply that they are all just talk.

"You're right. We didn't have any of those things. We invented them."

Reagan sugarcoated his barbs with humor, and this way he put humor to work for him.

*A heckler once tossed a cabbage at William Howard Taft during a political speech. He paused, peered at the vegetable, and then placidly said, "Ladies and Gentlemen, I see that one of my opponents has lost his head."

*Soon after he was elected governor, Reagan encountered a good deal of hostility in the press. He remarked, "If this has been a honeymoon, then I've been sleeping alone."

*When Sam Donaldson yelled over the noise of a helicopter on the South Lawn, "What about Walter Mondale's charges?" Ronald Reagan shot back, "He ought to pay for them."

*Politicians are persistently needled by the press. They pay back with humor. *The New York Times* and the *Washington Post* were often critical of President H. W. Bush's policies. When the White House announced the birth of puppies to Millie, George and Barbara Bush's beloved springer spaniel it led President Bush to gloat, "The puppies are sleeping on the *Washington Post* and *New York Times*. It's the first time in history these papers have been used to prevent leaks."

*When Will Hays accompanied Will Rogers to the White House to meet President Harding, Rogers said, "Mr. President, I would like to tell you all the latest political jokes."

"You don't have to, Will," Harding rejoined. "I appointed them."

*In the now well-known debate between Lincoln and Douglas, Douglas accused Lincoln of being two-faced. Lincoln's promptly fired back, "If I had two faces would I be wearing this one?"

*On his invitation to former Japanese Prime Minister Kiichi Miyazawa to attend a Bush Presidential Library function, President Bush quipped, "Some of you may remember him as the Japanese Prime Minister I threw up on," I told him, "This time, the dinner's on me."

Humor: Children's Weapon

Dear Mom and Dad,

I am sorry that I have not written, but all my stationery was destroyed when the dorm burned down. I am now out of the hospital and the doctor said that I will be fully recovered soon. I have also moved in with the boy who rescued me, since most of my things were destroyed in the fire.

Oh yes, I know that you have always wanted a grandchild, so you will be pleased to know that I am pregnant and you will have one soon.

Love, Mary.

Then—the postscript.

PS: There was no fire, my health is perfectly fine, and I am not pregnant. In fact, I do not even have a boyfriend.

However, I did get a D in French and a C in math and chemistry, and I just wanted to make sure that you keep it all in perspective.

Humor to Smooth Over Family Squabbles

Husband and wife have had a squabble the previous night. The wife was upset that she did not make up before the husband left for office in the morning. She opens her refrigerator, reaches for juice, and notices a pencil with a note on it stuck in the mound of leftover mashed potatoes. Her husband had written, "This is the way I feel. Please call me at the office when you wake up."

Humor to the Aid in Making Speeches

Humor is a great communicator. It helps to drive home a point and communicate truth and knowledge. As Samuel

Butler said, "A little levity will save many a good heavy thing from sinking." When the audience opens its mouth to laugh, you can drop a great rock of truth right in. Cicero, the legendary orator, used humor to great effect in public speaking. He relied on such tools as sarcasm, punning, and exaggeration.

*After a glowing introduction, the distinguished speaker stepped up to a podium, and a horrified audience watched helplessly as his written notes dropped from his hands, scattering across the floor. With the aid of the master of ceremonies, he took only a few moments to gather the papers. Silently, the lecturer rearranged his notes. Looked out at the audience and said, "For my next trick . . ."

*Billy Graham has overcome resistance on many occasions with an effective use of humor. He once addressed the student body of the prestigious London School of Economics, a university with decidedly left leanings. When he stood to speak to a packed auditorium, some booed. Shortly after he began to speak, a young man jumped out in front of the audience and began to heckle Billy Graham, acting like an ape, using gestures, scratching, and making noises like a monkey. As the student body roared with laughter, it seemed that the renowned preacher had lost his audience.

After a good hearty laugh of his own, Graham turned to his audience and said, "He reminds me of my ancestors." The hall was filled with laughter again. Then he said (here's the knockout punch), "Of course, all of my ancestors came from Britain."

Humor to the Rescue in Sales

It has the power to protect us from shame and embarrassment as you are going to see.

*A company representative was giving a group of visitors a tour around the factory. As they approached the testing department, a frustrated employee, unable to repair the part he was working on, picked it up and hauled it across the room. As the part hit the wall, the rep thoroughly embarrassed saved the day by proclaiming, "As you can see, all products are aerodynamically tested before leaving the factory . . ."

*In another incident, a salesman was demonstrating his company's machinery just as it malfunctioned. Rather than become all flustered, he recovered quickly and was the first to laugh at the failure. "Well, I guess that concludes my demonstration of my competitor's product for today. I'll be back tomorrow to show you ours."

*A woman regularly called on a business. After making her presentation, the buyer would politely say, "I'll call you if we need anything." She realized that he didn't remember her from one month to the next and never placed an order. Finally, she bought six helium-filled balloons and wrote both her name and her company's name on them.

This time when she walked into his office, she smiled and said, "Good morning," released the balloons, and left. The buyer, curiosity piqued, tracked her down for an explanation.

"I realize you're a busy man and have trouble telling one salesperson from another, so I thought I'd give you something to remember me by." The buyer laughed heartily and paid attention to her presentation. Then he wrote an order.

Humor as a Marketing Ploy in Ads

It involves making us laugh in order to make us buy.

The following are examples from *Humor in the Advertising Business* by Fred K. Beard.

*Nextel Dance Party boss asked three employees where someone else is. They are grooving and dancing to a boom-box. "No worry," they said and located him instantly vis-à-vis the Nextel tracking device. They resumed dancing.

*There were these three geeks practicing their hip-hop dancing in the office only to be interrupted by a panicked supervisor. "Where's the shipment?" and other questions. The geeks had split-second responses using Nextel technology, and then immediately went back to their hip-hop dance practice.

*Geeks were dancing in the office, boss entered demanding answers to three critical big problems. Music stopped, and they used their phones to get immediate answers, and went back to dancing.

Humor to Settle a Dispute

Don't lash out. Settle your difference with an effective humorous response.

My favorite

The couple had spent their honeymoon at a smart continental hotel. On the morning of their departure, the husband looked over the bill. "What is the meaning of this item—fruit, two hundred francs?" he demanded. "We haven't had any fruit."

"Quite," admitted the manager, "but fruit was placed on your table everyday while you were here. It was not the fault of the hotel that you did not eat it."

The husband counted out the amount due and then, looking the manager in the eye, said calmly, "I am deducting one hundred francs—for kissing my wife."

"Monsieur," cried the manager. "I have not ever kissed your wife."

"No?" said the husband. "But she was here. It isn't my fault if you didn't kiss her."

Humor as a Cure for a Serious Illness—the Medicinal Worth of Mirth

> A cheerful heart is a good medicine,
>
> But a downcast spirit dries up the bones. (Prov. 17: 22)

The healing power of laughter, happiness, and joy are acknowledged many times in the holy books of Christianity, Judaism, Hinduism, Islam, Sikhism, and Taoism.

Laughter is a pain antagonist. The seventeenth-century English physician Thomas Sydenham often referred to as the "English Hippocrates" caused wild consternation among his colleagues when he once said, "The arrival of a happy clown exercises a more beneficial influence upon the health of a town than twenty asses laden with drugs." One giggle is worth two tablets. "Comic relief," says Dr. Hunter Patch Adams, "is a major way for happy folk to dissipate pain. In a healthier world, humor would be a way of life. People would be funny as a rule, not an exception. One of the best aids in the transition from a 'heavy' to a 'light' existence is to open up the comedian in oneself."

*There is no better example in my opinion than the case of Norman Cousins. He was diagnosed as of having ankylosing spondylitis. Doctors gave him one chance in five hundred that he will be able to beat the illness. He did beat it. How did he do it? He put aside the large and often hazardous armamentarium of strong drugs whose side effects he was not certain of and placed his faith in self-reliance and the power of humor.

Let me quote from his book *Anatomy of an Illness*. "It was easy enough to hope and love and have faith, but what about laughter? Nothing is less funny than being flat on your back with all the bones in your spine and joints hurting. A systematic program was indicated. A good place to begin, I thought, was amusing movies. Allen Funt, producer of the spoofing television program *Candid Camera* sent films of his C. C. classics, along with a motion picture projector. The nurse was instructed in its use. We were even able to get our hands on some old Marx Brothers films. We pulled down the blinds and turned on the machine.

"It worked. *I made the joyous discovery that ten minutes of genuine belly laughter had an anesthetic effect and would give me at least two hours of pain-free sleep.* When the pain-killing effect of the laughter wore off, we would switch on the motion-picture projector again, and not infrequently, it would lead to another pain-free sleep interval. Sometimes, the nurse would read to me out of a trove of humor books."

Norman Cousins virtually laughed his way out of a crippling illness that doctors believed to be irreversible. He virtually mocked death with laughter and a positive attitude. Norman Cousins turned to humor to dispel fear and apprehension and to keep his spirits from sagging. He was healed by humor—that appreciating currency of hope. Humor was his novocaine, his penicillin.

*J. B. S. Haldane wrote a poem after a major operation for cancer, from which he subsequently died. The concluding stanza goes this way:

... *Provided one confronts the tumor*

With a sufficient sense of humor,

I know that cancer often kills

But so do cars and sleeping pills;

And it can hurt one till one sweats,

So can bad teeth and unpaid debts.

A spot of laughter, I am sure,

Often accelerates one's cure;

So let us patients do our bit

To help the surgeons make us fit.

*Dr. Albert Schweitzer the Peace Nobel laureate worked under very trying conditions in Lambarene, Africa. What kept them going was humor. Let Norman Cousins who knew Dr. Schweitzer take it from here. "Life for the young doctors and nurses was not easy at the Schweitzer Hospital. Dr. Schweitzer knew it and gave himself the task of supplying nutrients for their spirits. At mealtimes, when the staff came together, Schweitzer always had an amusing story or two to go with the meal. Laughter at the dinner hour was probably the most important course. It was fascinating to see the way the staff members seemed to be rejuvenated by the wryness of his humor. Humor at Lambarene was vital nourishment."

Perhaps it's pertinent to point out that chemists tell us that *happy people* produce *endorphins* and *enkephalins*—brain chemicals that improve T-cell production and thus enhance immunity to cancer, heart disease, and infections.

Humor to Dispel Fear

Paula, a twelve-year-old is visiting her grandparents in Florida. She likes to wade in the ocean but is afraid because she has just seen a movie about a killer shark. Her grandfather holds her hand as they approach the surf together and tells her gently, "I know you're worried, but remember, in this world there are more people eating fish than fish eating people." Both laugh.

Teaching of Religion through Humor

In the book *A Serious Discussion about Religion (but with a Touch of Humor)* by Reginald Dipwipple, I learnt that the commonality of all religions presented by the author was with not a touch as he claims but with a great deal of humor.

In this fictional presentation, the author was to meet a guy at a particular restaurant. He is on a secret mission. He gets caught in a shower and is drenched. For shelter, he enters a synagogue. "Amid the quiet interior," he writes, "I heard people talking in a nearby room." Here he meets four "people of cloth" (Jewish, Catholic, Muslim, and Buddhist) seated around a table.

He gets to talking to them killing time till the rain subsides. And from a series of questions and answers punctuated with humor, we learn that all religions say the same—"Love one another."

I give below excerpts:

> "So stranger—pray tell us your name and occupation." One of them wants to know. He worries, "My secret employer has ordered me not to divulge it." So he stutters, "Uuuuhh, I am in the process of changing my name"—because I'm always in the process of changing my name—"but you can call me Sigmund."
>
> "You're changing your name? Why? Do you work on Wall Street? Broadway?"
>
> The Rabbi who was doing the talking opened a book that was lying on the table and finding the page he wanted, he slid the book over to Sigmund and the English text reads:

"On judgment Day every person will be called to account for every permissible thing he might have enjoyed but did not."

Oh God what a relief, he thinks.

"Thank you, Rabbi. This is very interesting. I always thought that comedy was sacrilegious. After all, it makes people happy. So what is this book?"

"Part of the Talmud."

"The what?"

"The Talmud. It's a collection of ancient rabbinical writings on Jewish law and tradition. It's so vast, there's something for everybody. For example, one rabbi's contribution reads, 'Tongue in the mouth of a woman is one of God's less agreeable blunders.'"

"I'll bet that guy was a polygamist," remarked the Buddhist nun.

" . . . I'm curious, what does Buddhism teach?"

"Well, Sigmund, Buddhism teaches that a person's emotional attachment to material things and to worldly desires ultimately results in one's suffering. Real happiness comes from within . . ."

"Hummm. Do Buddhists believe in humor?"

"Oh, of course! Buddhists love paradox. For instance, Buddhists are fulfilled by emptiness. The Lord Buddha himself said, 'I gained nothing at all from Supreme Enlightenment, and for that reason it is called Supreme Enlightenment.' In my own case, a Zen master once told me to 'do the opposite of whatever I tell you.' So I didn't."

"Sigmund," said the Imam, "in Islam especially in the Sunni tradition, we have the Hadith. The Hadith are books containing thousands of narratives about the words and deeds of the Prophet Mohammed. Peace and blessings be upon him. From those narratives we know that the Prophet smiled, he laughed, he even told jokes. One narrative tells us an old widow asked a prophet if there are old women in heavenly paradise. He answered no. That answer really scared her—until it was explained to her that when old women enter paradise, God restores them to youth."

"I like that."

"In the Shi'a tradition of Islam, there is a book we call the Nahjul Balagha. One of its sayings tells us, 'Treat people in such a way and live among them in such a manner that, if you die, they will weep over you. Alive, they will crave your company.' Islam also teaches that you shouldn't laugh at somebody who is in desperate need of charity. But that doesn't mean playfulness is always wrong, or that we should never laugh."

"Gosh. That sounds very profound. However, speaking as a comedy writer, I'll take any laughs I can get, whatever the reason. To me that's charity. Father Francisco, what can you say to me about humor in Christianity?"

"Well, Sigmund I'm convinced that Jesus told jokes."

"You are? Why?"

"The Gospels imply as much. Jesus said things like, 'Why do you seek the speck in your neighbor's eye but not the log in your own eye?' The Gospels also say that Jesus attended parties. His first recorded miracle was at a party, where he turned water into wine. If a party's worth of Divine wine doesn't encourage joke-telling, what does? The Gospel of John declares that if everything Jesus said and did had been recorded in detail, the whole world couldn't hold all the books. Well, if Jesus did that much and I'm sure he did, then I can't believe he never told a joke."

Do you know any jokes yourself Father?

"Well, the other day God sneezed. I didn't know what to say to Him. But I think the biggest joke in Christianity is actually on us Christians because it took a devout Hindu to show Christians the power of Christian love, expressed as nonviolence."

"What a Hindu?"

"Yes, Mohandas Gandhi and his followers used nonviolent resistance to gain India's independence in 1947, after centuries of foreign rule. Gandhi openly admitted that he was persuaded to nonviolence after reading Jesus's Sermon on the Mount. 'Love your enemies; bless those who curse you; do good to those who hate you.' Decades later, in the 1960s, the Reverend Martin Luther King and his followers applied Gandhi's tactics against racial segregation in the South, and they transformed America for the better."

"Gosh. Really?"

"Yes. Nonviolence works by shaming the bullies into backing down. Otherwise everything that the bullies stand for, their self-proclaimed model society, becomes a joke.

"You know, Sigmund," said the Imam, "while Gandhi was waging his campaign of nonviolence in India, similar campaign was being waged in what is today Pakistan by a devout Muslim named Gaffer-Khan. Gaffer-Khan was inspired by the Holy Quran, the central book of Islam. The Quran tells us that 'those who act kindly in this world will have kindness.' Gaffer-Khan and Gandhi were even friends. Today, anybody who thinks that Islam cannot inspire peaceful activism or tolerance or justice, I say they should study Gaffer-Khan."

" . . . When he was asked what is the best thing in Islam, the Prophet answered, 'It is to feed the hungry and give the greeting of peace to both'—to those one knows and to those one does not know."

Sigmund: "But before I make a moral decision, do I have to read the entire Bible?"

"Fortunately, the wisest religious sages in history have an answer for you. It's called the Golden Rule."

"The Golden Rule? He who owns the gold rules?"

"No Sigmund. I mean the Golden Rule as exemplified by the wisdom of Hillel the Elder."

"Who?"

"Hillel the Elder, one of the wisest of Jewish scholars. In ancient Jerusalem, Hillel was once met by a stranger who had a question. Before the stranger asked it, however, he grabbed his own foot to balance himself on one leg. In that precarious position the stranger then asked Hillel to summarize in just a few seconds the entirety of Biblical morality and wisdom. Well, Hillel did. He answered, 'What is hateful to you, do not do to your fellow man." "This is the entire law. The rest is commentary—go study."

Sigmund: "Follow the Golden Rule. Isn't that kinda trite?"

"It may be trite" said Dharma, "but the Golden rule exists in every major religion in the world. Sigmund, I just happen to have here"—she reached into a small purse she carried and pulled out a piece of paper—"a list that proves it. Here."

Judaism: "What is hateful to you, do not do to your fellow man."

Christianity: "Do unto others as you would have them do unto you."

Islam: "No one of you is a believer until he desires for his brother what he desires for himself."

Buddhism: "Hurt not others in ways that you yourself would find hurtful."

Hinduism: "This is the sum of duty: do not unto others that would cause pain if done unto you."

Confucianism: Do not do to others what you would not like done to yourself."

Taoism: Regard your neighbor's gain as your own, and your neighbor's loss as your own loss."

Sigmund: Thank you, all of you. I'd love to stay longer, but I need to go."

"Sigmund, if you want a nice lunch, don't go to Smoky's. A little ways down the street is a great Jewish deli called Manna. It's run by my brother.

"I'd love to, but—hey, wait a minute. Rabbi, didn't you say that you eat at Smoky's all the time?"

"Yes."

"Then why don't you eat at your own brother's deli?"

"Because he's a schmuck. But it is a great deli."

"Speaking of lunch, Rabbi, when are you going to start eating ham?"

"At your wedding, Father."

*Christ taught serious morals through the use of humor in hyperbole. In what is called discourse on judgmentalism, which is part of the Sermon on the Mount, he directs the faithful the proper way of forming opinion of others—first, amend your own fault. He says it with a touch of humor employing hyperbole. "Cast out the *beam (large beam of wood)* out of thine eye and then shalt thou see clearly to cast out the mote (any small dry body) out of thy brother's eye." We pay too much attention to detail (the letter of the law) and treat cavalierly the weightier matters such as mercy, service, and loving one another—"You strain," he admonishes, "*a gnat* (out of your wine)" and again hyperbole to drive home the point, "but swallow a *camel.*"

*I tell you the truth; it is hard for a rich man to enter the kingdom of heaven. Again I tell you, it is easier for a *camel* (using amusing hyperbole) *to go through the eye of a needle* than for a rich man to enter the kingdom of God. (Matt. 19: 23-24)

The saying was a response to a young rich man who had asked what he needed to do in order to attain eternal life. Jesus replied that he should keep the commandments, to which the man stated he had done. Jesus responded, "If you want to be perfect, go and sell your possessions and give to the poor, and you will have treasure in heaven. Then, come follow me." The young man became sad and was unwilling to do this. Jesus then spoke this response, leaving his disciples astonished. (Matt. 19: 16-24)

Humor to Handle an Awkward Social Comment

The following extracts are from Jon Mack's *How to Be Funny*.

A new biography about Sandy Koufax by Jane Leavy discusses how difficult it was for him as one of the few Jewish players in the majors. (And of course there are so many now.) The author cited two examples of him using jokes to lighten an awkward situation. The first involved a time they had a party at Duke Snider's house. There was a pig roast in the backyard, and Snider's wife was concerned about what Sandy would eat. He pointed to the pig and said, "I'll have some of that turkey."

Another time Koufax was on a bus going through Miami when one of the Dodger coaches yelled out, "You can give this damn town back to the Jews." Koufax said, "Billy, we already own it." Both approaches worked. One was a kind and funny way of easing tension, the other used the hidden truth to make a point.

Humor as a Teaching Tool

A *Quaker* is trying to harness his lone mule to plow a rocky field. The donkey bites him. The *Quaker* tries again. The donkey kicks him in the stomach. Finally, the man gets the animal hooked to the plow, and the donkey turns and runs the plow over the *Quaker's* foot.

Pushed beyond human endurance, the gentle Quaker limps around to the donkey's face, holds him nose to nose, and says, "Thou knowest I shall not strike thee, friend ass. Thou knowest I shall not curse thee, either. But what thou doesn't knowest is that I can sell thee to the Southern Baptist down the road."

The kindly Quaker despite all the mule-kicks he received, he retained his *sense of humor*.

Humor in Parables

Parables are stories which serve to illustrate a moral point. They have a clear joke structure in them, complete with punch lines. Many parables are religious in nature and can be found in religious texts such as the Bible or the Buddhist Tripitaka. There are also secular parables, including those in Aesop's Fables, such as "The Boy Who Cried Wolf." Parables with a coloring of humor can be an effective way to impart moral teachings, as humorous stories can be recalled with clarity and interest and are often more memorable than other teaching tools.

*Through humorous parables valid lessons are imparted to children. "The Boy Who Cried Wolf" in Aesop's Fables warns against lying because of its inevitable consequences. This story has become part of common vernacular. The boy, a sheepherder, was bored while guarding the sheep on a hill, so he cried out that a wolf was attacking the sheep. The villagers rushed over, only to find out that the boy had lied to them. The boy cried out a second time, with the same results. And when a real wolf came to devour the sheep, and the boy cried out, the villagers ignored his cries with tragic results. Children are taught the lesson—a liar will seldom be believed even when telling the truth.

*"The Emperor's New Clothes" is a parable with a touch of humor. It's about people's unwillingness to call attention to something wrong for fear of looking foolish. A vain emperor who enjoyed wearing all sorts of fancy clothes was approached by two con artists who tell him that they will create for him a suite of clothes that is invisible to stupid or incompetent people. The emperor pays the men to create the clothes, though in actuality they create nothing at all and only pretend to work on the suit. Everyone admires the clothes for fear of being seen as stupid or incompetent. The emperor ends up taking off his clothes to try on the pair of invisible clothes and ends up parading naked around town. The only person who calls attention to the emperor being naked is a young boy in the streets. "Look," he says, "the emperor has no clothes."

All Is Vanity

All is Vanity is a Buddhist parable about how humans should forsake worldly pleasures and attempt to lead a life without temptation or suffering. In "All Is Vanity," a rare species of monkeys lived in the Himalayas. Hunters set a trap to capture the monkeys because they wished to collect their prized rare blood. The monkeys were clever and skilled at avoiding traps but couldn't resist rice wine and fancy shoes, so the hunters set up a trap with rice wine barrels and dancing clogs. The monkeys saw it was a trap but still couldn't resist drinking the wine and dancing in the shoes, and the hunters captured and killed them. The parable illustrates how people often give in to temptation even if they know it is bad for them.

Never Underestimate Anyone

Avvaiyar was a highly educated and respected lady poet throughout India. The king would leave the throne and go up to receive her. No one in the land could match her debating skills. She therefore, as to be expected, became very arrogant.

One hot day, she was resting under a naval tree and became thirsty. She noticed a shepherd boy seated on the branch of the tree and eating naval fruits. She asked him to throw some for her and the boy inquired whether she wanted regular fruits or hot ones. Avvaiyar laughed (how come there are hot fruits on the tree), and in order to go with the flow of the fun, said, "Throw me some very hot ones." The boy plucked some very ripe fruits and threw them in the sand. The old lady picked the fruits and began blowing the sand away. The little boy perched on the tree called out, "Are they very hot, Patti (Grandma)?" She suddenly realized what the boy meant by a "hot fruit." She felt humiliated at being outwitted by a little boy.

Let Not Greed Come in the Way of Your Goal

Once upon a time, there lived a beautiful and charming princess in Greece. She was not only beautiful but also adept in shooting, hunting, and running. In fact, she had earned the title of "the fleet-footed princess." Many handsome and heroic princes desired to win her heart and hand. So the princess hit upon a clever plan. She announced that she would marry the young man who would beat her in a footrace. Hundreds of young warriors came to race with her, but she would always beat them.

At last, one young hero was determined to beat her. He sought the advice of a wise man. He explained to him about the fleet-footed princess and her challenge. He also expressed his regret over the fact that many young warriors were being put to shame by the princess.

The wise man hit upon a plan. "Take," he said, "in your pocket several shining pieces of jewelry and gems. As you run, go on dropping one piece after another on the racing track at strategic points."

On the day fixed for the race, the young man equipped himself with fine pieces of jewelry. The young man and the princess started running. Both of them were good runners. Whenever the princess was about to overtake, the young man would deftly drop a dazzling piece of jewelry. The princess spontaneously stopped to pick up the lovely piece of jewelry that was on the racing track. She was confident in spite of the halts that she would be able to outrun her rival. These brief but frequent halts made him reach the goal ahead of her. Thus the young man won the race as well as the heart and the hand of the princess.

Parable of the Elephant and the Blind Men

One person does not have all the answers.

Humor we see being used to entertain and educate.

A king has the blind men of the capital brought to the palace, where an elephant is brought in, and they are asked to describe it.

When the blind men had each felt a part of the elephant, the king went to each of them and asked, "Well, blind man, have you seen the elephant? Tell me, what sort of thing is an elephant?"

The men assert that the elephant is either like a pot (the blind man who felt the elephant's head), a winnowing basket (ear), a ploughshare (tusk), a plow (trunk), a pillar (foot), or a brush (tip of the tail), depending on what part of the elephant each blind man had felt.

The men cannot agree and come to blows, at which point the king intervenes and tells them that they are all correct in parts. Their knowledge put together gives the truth.

And so these men of Hindustan

Disputed loud and long,

Each in his own opinion

Exceeding stiff and strong,

Though each was partly in the right

And all were in the wrong."

The moral:

So oft in theologic wars,

The disputants, I ween,

Of what each other mean,

And prate about an Elephant

Not one of them has been or seen.

(John Godfrey Saxe)

We learn from St. Augustine: "Let us on both sides lay aside all arrogance; let us not on either side, claim—we have already discovered the truth."

The Book of Proverbs Using Humorous Exaggeration

*Like an archer who wounds everybody is one who hires a passing fool or drunkard. (Prov. 26: 10)

*Like a dog that returns to its vomit is a fool who reverts to his folly. (Prov. 26: 11)

*The lazy person says, "There is a lion in the road! There is a lion in the streets." (Prov. 26: 13)

*As a door turns on its hinges, so does a lazy person in bed. (Prov. 26: 14)

*The lazy person buries a hand in the dish and is too tired to bring it back to the mouth. (Prov. 26: 15)

Humor Teaches Us that Everything Is Not What Appears to Be

According to a Nigerian legend, there used to be a trickster and a troublemaker who went under various names—Edshu, Eshu, Lega, or Elegba. He was a homeless wanderer. One day, he was walking on the path between two fields. He saw a farmer in each field and decided to play a trick on them. Putting on a hat that was red on one side and white on the other, green in front, and black at the back, he walked down a path between the fields of the two farmers, who were lifelong friends. Later, the friends quarreled about the old man who had walked past, one saying his cap was white and the other that it was red. The quarrel grew to such an extent that the friends came to blows, the neighbors had to intervene, and the disputants were taken to the headman. While the two former friends accused one another of lying, Eshu announced that neither of them were liars, but both were fools and admitted his role in the story. The headman was very angry and tried to have Eshu arrested, but he managed to escape, setting fire to houses on his way. As people carried their belongings out of the burning houses, Eshu offered to look after them, but instead of doing so, he gave them away to passers-by.

Humor to Steel Your Resolve Not to Succumb

Saint Lawrence was one of seven deacons who were in charge of giving help to the poor and needy. When a persecution broke out, Pope St. Sixtus was condemned to death. As he was led to execution, Lawrence followed him weeping. "Father, where are you going without your deacon?" asked Saint Lawrence. "I am not leaving you, my son," answered the Pope. "In three days, you will follow me." Full of joy, Lawrence gave to the poor the rest of the money he had on hand and even sold expensive vessels to have more to give away.

The prefect of Rome, a greedy man, thought the church had a great fortune hidden away. So he ordered Lawrence to bring the church's treasure to him. The saint said he would bring it in three days. Then he went through the city and gathered together all the poor and sick people supported by the church. When he showed them to the prefect, he said, "This is the church's treasure!"

In great anger, the prefect condemned Lawrence to a slow, cruel death. The saint was tied on top of an iron grill over a slow fire that roasted his flesh little by little, but Lawrence, undeterred, joked, "Turn me over," he said to the judge, "I'm done on this side!" And just before he died, he said, "It's cooked enough now."

Mean-spirited, cruel people use humor to ridicule and humiliate. This is the dark underbelly of humor.

Here are a few examples:

*Joking person (JP): Ha-ha-ha-ha, that sweater is so ugly! It makes you look huge. Ha-ha-ha-ha.

Not-amused person (NA): Um . . . Excuse me?

JP: Oh, don't get offended. It was just a joke! Don't be so sensitive.

*JP: Ha-ha-ha . . . I hate working with women. God, they are so stupid and so petty. Ha-ha-ha.

NA: Um, what? Did you actually just say that?

JP: Geez, I was just kidding. Lighten up! How come no one has a *sense of humor* these days?

*JP: Ha-ha-Ha-black people are so ridiculous. I mean, do you see the way they dress or the way they wear their hair? Ha-ha-ha.

NA: What the hell did you just say?

JP: I was just kidding. You need to learn to take a joke. Political correctness is such bullshit. What a bunch of crybabies!

Humor as a Way to Impose Social Discipline

Humor serves to keep immigrants in place until they learn how to behave like Americans. Immigrants take extra pains to study earnestly and expeditiously the local customs, slangs, and manner of speaking so as not to be at the receiving end of cruel jokes. Here are a couple of examples:

What has the IQ of 144? Answer: A gross of Irishman.

And this one: A man is disgusted by the state of his Pakistani neighbor's dustbin. He goes next door and speaks to the head of the household. "Look here," he says, "I've come about your dustbin." "I'm very sorry sir," says the polite Pakistani householder, "it's already let."

The German was teased for his "dumb" rural ways, the Irishman for his blarney, and the Scot for his thrift.

Turning Sour to Sweet

Once, during the dark days of the Civil War, Secretary of War Stanton called Lincoln "a damn fool" in the presence of Mr. Lovejoy of Illinois. When the enraged Lovejoy reported this to the president, Lincoln said, "Did Stanton call me a damn fool?" and was thoughtful for a moment. "Well, I guess I had better step over and see Stanton about this. Stanton is usually right." In this way, Lincoln eased a delicate situation.

Humor as a Way to Challenge the Ability of Death to Demoralize Us

Humor is one method that we have at our disposal for taking some of the sting out of death. Humor, properly employed, can serve as a balm instead of a bomb.

We see this detailed elsewhere as *Gallows Humor.* "You can kill me but you cannot hurt me" (referring to his personality and pride) is the underlying theme. Here are a couple of examples from Freud.

*A criminal who was being led to the place of execution asked for a scarf for his bare throat so as not to catch a cold.

*A criminal who is being led to the gallows on a Monday morning quips, "Well, this is a good beginning to the week."

Humor to get even. Don't lash out; laugh it off.

He Swears He'll Come Back to Haunt Her

An elderly Italian man, Uncle Vito, and woman, Juliana, were married for years even though they hated each other. When they had a confrontation, screams and yelling could be heard deep into the night. A constant statement was heard by the neighbors who feared the man the most. "When I die, I will dig my way up and out of the grave to come back and haunt you for the rest of your life!"

They believed he practiced black magic and was responsible for missing cats and dogs and strange sounds at all hours. He was feared and enjoyed the respect it garnished.

He died abruptly under strange circumstances, and the funeral had a closed casket. After the burial, the wife went straight to the local bar and began to party as if there was no tomorrow.

The gaiety of her actions becoming extreme, her neighbors approached in a group to ask these questions: Are you not worried? Concerned? Aren't you afraid of this man who practiced black magic and stated when he died he would dig his way up and out of the grave to come back and haunt you for the rest of your life?

Juliana put down her drink and said, "Let the old bastard dig his way out. I had him buried upside down."

The Usher's Revenge

A man takes his seat in the theater, but he is too far from the screen. He whispers to the usher, "This is a mystery, and I have to watch a mystery close-up. Get me a better seat, and I'll give you a handsome tip."

The usher moves him into the second row, and the man rewards him with a dollar.

The usher looks at his tip for a second and then leans over to whisper to the man, "The wife did it."

Bride and Best Man Exposed

This is a true story about a recent wedding that took place at Clemson University, commented by Jay Leno.

It was a wedding with about three hundred guests. After the wedding, at the reception, the groom got up on stage with a microphone to talk to the crowd. He said that he wanted to thank everyone for coming, many from long distances, to support them at their wedding. He especially wanted to thank the bride's and groom's families for coming and to thank his new father-in-law for providing such a fabulous reception.

He said he wanted to give everyone a special gift from just him. So taped to the bottom of everyone's chair was a manila envelope. He said that this was a gift to everyone and told everyone to open the envelopes. Inside each manila envelope was an 8 × 10 picture of his best man in "compromising" positions with his bride.

He had gotten suspicious of the two of them and hired a private detective to trail them weeks prior to the wedding. After he stood there and watched the people's reactions for a couple of minutes, he turned to the best man and said, "Fiddle . . . you!" He turned to his bride and said, "Fiddle . . . you!" and then he turned to the dumbfounded crowd and said, "I'm out of here." He had the marriage annulled first thing that Monday morning. While most of us would have broken off the engagement immediately after finding out about the affair, this guy goes through with it anyway, as if nothing was wrong.

His revenge: Making the bride's parents pay over $32,000 for three hundred guests for a wedding and reception. Letting everyone know exactly what did happen.

Solving the Spilled Coffee Problem

The young clerk's responsibilities included bringing the judge a hot cup of coffee at the start of everyday.

Each morning, the judge was enraged that the coffee cup arrived two-thirds full. The clerk explained that he had to rush to get the coffee delivered while it was still hot, which caused him to spill much of it along the way.

None of the judge's yelling and insults produced a full cup of coffee, until he finally threatened to cut the clerk's pay by one-third if he continued to produce one-third less than the judge wanted.

The next morning, he was greeted with a cup of coffee that was full to the brim and the next morning and the morning after that.

The judge couldn't resist gloating over his success and smugly complimented the clerk on his new technique.

"Oh, there's not much to it," admitted the clerk happily, "I just sip some coffee right outside the coffee room and spit it back in when I get outside your office."

One-dollar Beer

A man walked into a bar one night. He went up to the bar and asked for a beer.

"Certainly, sir, that'll be dollar."

"One dollar!" exclaimed the guy.

The barman replied, "Yes."

So the guy glanced over the menu, and he asked, "Could I have a nice juicy T-bone steak with fries, peas, and a salad?"

"Certainly, sir," replied the bartender, "but all that comes to real money."

"How much money?" the guy asked.

"Three dollars," he replied.

"Three dollars!" exclaimed the guy. "Where's the guy who owns this place?"

The barman replied, "Upstairs with my wife."

The guy said, "What's he doing with your wife?"

The bartender replied, "Same as what I'm doing to his business."

Mother of Six

A man has six children and is very proud of his achievement. He is so proud of himself that he starts calling his wife "Mother of Six" in spite of her objections.

One night, they go to a party. The man decides that it's time to go home and wants to find out if his wife is ready to leave as well.

He shouts at the top of his voice, "Shall we go home now, Mother of Six?"

His wife, irritated by her husband's lack of discretion, shouts back, " . . . Anytime you're ready, Father of Four."

Budweiser Please

A visitor was taken round the "The Boston Beer Company" brewery. Proudly, the guide showed him how the various brands, the Boston Lager, Sam Adams Light, Porch Rocker, Summer Ale, were brewed. At the end of the tour, the guide asked the visitor which brand he would like to taste. The visitor, with a broad grin, said, "May I have a glass of Budweiser please?"

Unabashed, the guide said, "No Problem," filled a glass with tap water, and gave it to him.

> Like merry Momus, while the Gods were quaffing,
>
> I come to give a Eulogy on Laughing.
>
> But, in the main, tho' laughing I approve,
>
> It is not every kind of laugh I love;
>
> For many laughs even candor must condemn,
>
> Some are too full of acid, some of phlegm.
>
> The honest laugh, unstudied, un-acquired,

By nature prompted and true wit inspired,

Alone deserves the applauding Muse's grace;

The rest is all contortion and grimace.

But should my feeble efforts move your glee,

Laugh, if you fairly can—but not at me!

(Excerpt from *Eulogy on Laughing* by J. M. Sewall)

Just Kidding

No book on humor will be complete without a collection of jokes. You may have heard some of them before but had forgotten them until now. You may not mind hearing them again. Broadly, jokes can be classified under two categories: (a) purely topical or provincial as to time and place and (b) timeless and universal. The universal is understood by everyone, even when translated out of the language of origin. The provincial or topical generally requires supplementary comments to greater understanding. In this chapter, as in the rest of the book, I have endeavored to embrace both domains.

A joke is a compressed short story. The mainstream belief is that there are really no new jokes. Each one is a take-off on an old joke. The specific content may vary but structure-wise they are the same. Old wine in new bottles can be exhilarating too. This example elucidates my point of view. At one time, different parts of the body argued as to which of them is the most important. The argument was finally won by the anus, who pointed out that if it chose to cease functioning, everyone else will have to shut down. This joke strangely has an antecedent in the New Testament, specifically, in the First Epistle of the Corinthians, wherein, after considering the relative merits of the different body parts, Paul concludes that "God has so adjusted the body, giving the greater honor to the inferior part," a part which despite its usefulness is "unpresentable." Jokes too have their seasons. Many of them tend to flourish for a while and then fade away. They are culture and time bound. Be they old or new, it's always fun to read them and wherever possible recall and relate them in the company of friends. For a joke to give pleasure, it needs to be shared. Like misery, hilarity too loves company. Smart people mix into the ebb and flow of friendly conversation and communication—jokes that they feel will liven up their friends. Sharing a joke with someone is a roundabout way of telling that person I like you. It is by sharing our stories, jokes, and anecdotes that we become one community.

Jokes have an interesting history. According to anthropologist Max Gluckman, the hunting Esquimaux of the Arctic Circle used jokes in place of a court system; they governed their society through humorous insult contests called drumming matches. This was in the early sixties. When disputes arose, they were settled in formal song duels where each side would insult the other as devastatingly and hilariously as possible, judgment being given in the form of audience applause and laughter. Fancy the US Supreme Court deciding Roe vs. Wade in like manner. *Justice Clarence Thomas et al.*

Clean jokes, not cruel jibes, obscene quips, the kind I have to look over the shoulder before repeating them, promote intimacy and camaraderie. A handful of cracks can always be depended upon to create a climate to make individuals comfortable with each other. A good joke is footloose; it takes a life of its own as it passes from person to person, through a playground, pub, or e-mail.

Almost no collection of jokes has ever been published in any language, in the exact words, in which they were told. Jokes are not invented; they evolve and they arrive to us from other countries and older civilizations, by way of oral and printed infiltrations over a period of centuries. People on the Internet today have no idea that jokes they are trading are hundreds of years old. It is believed if Adam should visit earth, the only thing he would probably recognize would be the jokes. Some believe jokes emanate from stockbrokers, who have time on their hands between sales and a communication network to send them around and from prisoners who have a lot of spare time and an ever-ready captive audience.

Not every joke in this collection will cause all the pleasant reactions I would like to see. Some of your favorites may not be even here. The reason being (a) times change and taste changes with them and (b) in spite of a lifetime spent enjoying reading and swapping jokes, it is possible that I've never encountered your particular favorite. Jay Leno reviews fifteen hundred jokes everyday before whittling them down to fifteen and yet some to his chagrin pratfall. If you do not like a joke, you can fast-forward the way we do with pesky commercials.

I have sought out popular jokes that circulate and so feel no obligation to document their provenance. Remember the jokes here serve as the hors d'oeuvre, the accompaniment to the meal, not the meal itself. Jokes are not things that are pulled out of midair or nowhere but those that we hear, remember, and retell.

It is famously said that when a Frenchman hears a joke, he always laughs three times—first when he hears it, second when you explain it to him, and third when he understands. That is because a Frenchman likes to laugh. When you tell a joke to an Englishman, he laughs twice—once when you tell it and a second time when you explain it to him. When you tell a joke to a German, he only laughs once, that is, when you tell it to him. He won't let you explain it to him because he is too arrogant. When you tell a joke to a Jew—before you finish it, he interrogates you. First, he has heard it before; second, you are not telling it right; and third, he ends up telling you the story the way it should be told. Wittgenstein once said that he could imagine a book of philosophy being written entirely in the form of jokes.

Humans are the only species that have been endowed with the gift of laughter. So let's make the most of it.

"Feast often and use friends not still so sad,

Whose jests and merriment may make thee glad." (EO Bannus Hessus.)

The way I see it, jokes work like boxing. The boxer keeps jabbing the opponent with his left, biding his time, and when the opponent least expects it, brings him down with a right hook, only in this case no one gets hurt. You will see what I mean.

A cowboy rides into town and stops at the saloon. However, when he's finished his drink, he goes out to find his horse's stolen. The cowboy walks back into the bar, loosens his guns on their holster, and says, "I'm gonna have another beer, and if my horse ain't back outside by the time I'm finished, I'm gonna do what I dun in Texas" The cowboy has his drink and goes back to find his horse back where he left it. Up to this point it's very matter-of-fact, let's say he's been jabbing with is left. *Now for the knockout punch.*

The bartender calls out after him, "Hey, partner, what exactly happened in Texas?"

The cowboy says, "I had to walk home."

A cautionary note:

In order to be able to get maximum bounce for the ounce certain jokes must be heard rather than read. The following is a good illustration.

*In *My Little Chickadee*, there is a scene in which Fields is about to be lynched outside a western saloon. He is asked if he has a last request before being hanged.

"Yes," says Fields, "I'd like to see Paris before I die." The mob, not amused at all, calls for the hangman to get on with it and string him up, and as the noose is tightened, Fields says, "Philadelphia will do."

The ability to laugh and enjoy jokes can be a measuring tape of our state of mind. If we can laugh at the slapstick antics of the three stooges, we are childlike with a passport to heaven, but if we think of them as silly, in my opinion, we have sadly become frosty and fossil-like. Need not be so.

Let's see how we make out.

*An impoverished man borrowed twenty-five dollars from a well-to-do acquaintance, assuring him at some length of his distress. On the very same day, his patron comes upon him in a restaurant with a plate of salmon with mayonnaise before him. He reproaches him:

"What, you borrow money from me and then you go and order salmon with mayonnaise. That's what you used my money for?"

"I don't get it," answers the accused, "when I've got no money, I can't eat salmon with mayonnaise. When I've got money, I mustn't eat salmon with mayonnaise. So tell me, when can I eat salmon with mayonnaise?"

*A cowboy had two horses, but he couldn't tell them apart. He cut off one horse's mane, but it grew back. A friend suggested that he measure the horses. The cowboy measured them, went to his friend and said, "That was a great idea—the black one was two inches taller than the white one."

*Three mice are sitting around boasting about their strengths. The first mouse says, "Mousetraps are nothing! I do push-ups with the bar."

The second mouse pulls a pill from his pocket, swallows it, and says with a grin, "That was rat poison."

The third mouse got up to leave. The first mouse asks, "Where do you think you're going?"

"It's time to go home and chase the cat."

*First cowboy: "Why did you carry only one log for the campfire when the other hands carry two?"

Second cowboy: "I guess the others are too lazy to make two trips."

*A site foreman had ten very lazy men working for him, so one day, he decided to trick them into doing some work for a change.

"I've a really easy job today for the laziest one among you," he announced. "Will the laziest man please raise his hand?"

Nine hands shot up.

"Why didn't you put your hand up?" he asked the tenth man.

"It was too much trouble."

*Waiter: And how did you find your steak, sir?

Customer: Well, I pushed aside a bean and there it was.

*A police officer was escorting a prisoner to jail when the officer's hat blew off down the sidewalk.

"Would you like me to get that for you?" asked the prisoner.

"You must think I am an idiot," said the officer. "You just wait here, and I'll get it."

*"Mr. Churchill, I care neither for your politics nor your moustache."

"Do not distress yourself, madam, you are unlikely to come into contact with either."

*A very nervous young man came in with a girl to get a marriage license and the clerk, taking down the data, murmured, "Parent's consent?"

"Parent's consent," he said. "Who the hell do you think that is in the door with a shotgun, Daniel Boone?"

*A woman got on the train with nine children, and when the conductor came for her tickets, she said, "Now these three are thirteen years old and pay full fare, but those three over there are only six, and these three here four and a half" The conductor looked at her in amazement.

"Do you mean to say you get three every time?" he asked.

"Oh no," she said, "sometimes we don't get any at all."

*A feminist gets on a bus and is disgusted when a little old man stands up to give her his seat. "Patronizing old fool," she mutters as she pushes him back down. A minute later, another woman gets on, and the old man rises to his feet once more. "Male chauvinist pig," seethes the feminist as she pushes him back down again. The bus stops again and more women get on; once more the little old man attempts to stand up. "You are living in the Stone Age," hisses the feminist as she pushes him down. "For God's sake!" wails the little old man. "Will you let me get off? I've missed three stops already."

*The King of Jordan visits London and is invited to dinner with the Queen. The servants bring out the first course and start dishing out. "No soup for me," says the King of Jordan. "It makes me fart." Silence falls over the room. Everyone is horrified. "What's the matter with you all?" asks the King, patting his belly. "Don't you think I'm fart enough already!"

*A wife hears a noise in the kitchen one morning. She goes downstairs and finds her husband slumped at the table stinking of booze and with lipstick stains all over his shirt.

"I hope you've got a good reason for being here at seven in the morning," she glowers.

"I certainly do," replies her husband, "Breakfast."

*It is not true that she dyes her hair black. It was black when she bought it.

*Grandma finally figured out how to stop Grandpa chasing after other women—she let the air out of his wheelchair tires.

*A man walks into a bar and sits down next to an old drunk. He smells a foul odor, turns to the drunk, and says, "Jesus! Did you crap in your pants?" "Yup," replies the drunk. "Then why don't you go to the bathroom?" asks the man. The drunk replies, "'Cause I ain't finished yet."

*A cowboy comes out of a saloon and finds that someone has painted his horse with whitewash. He storms back inside and shouts, "Which one of you bastards whitewashed my horse?" A huge gunslinger stands up and says, "Me. Why'd you want to know?" "No reason," says the cowboy. "Just thought I'd tell you the first coat is dry."

*Some cannibals get a job in a big corporation on condition they don't eat any of the other staff.

Things go very well until their boss calls them into his office and tells them—an office cleaner is missing in mysterious circumstances, and the cannibals are under suspicion. The cannibals get together after work. The leader says, "Which of you idiots had the cleaner?" One of the cannibals raises his hand. "You idiots, for weeks, we've been feasting on team leaders, project managers, and human resources staff, then you go and eat someone they'll actually miss."

*A salesman rings the doorbell of a house. The door is answered by a young boy smoking a cigar, holding a glass of brandy, with a copy of Playboy tucked under his arm. "Say, sonny," says the salesman. "Is your mother at home?" The boy taps the ash off his cigar and says, "What the hell do you think?"

*Harry is in the middle of a speech when someone at the back calls out, "I can't hear you." Someone at the front calls back, "Could we swap places?"

*A guest speaker is trying to make himself heard over the racket of a boisterous rugby club dinner. He complains to the president sitting next to him, "It's too noisy. I can't hear myself speak." "Please, don't worry about it," replies the president. "You're not missing anything."

*A boss approaches his four employees and tells them he has to fire one of them. The black employee replies, "I'm a protected minority." The female employee replies, "And I'm a woman." The oldest employee says, "Fire me, buster, and I'll hit you with age-discrimination suit." Every one turns to look at the young white guy. He thinks for a moment then says, "I think I might be gay."

*"Do you want gas?" the dentist asked as the absent-minded patient sat down in the chair. "Yes," replied the absent-minded one. "Five gallons please and check the oil too."

*A Westchester college student lad returned from a vacation in Europe to announce to his mother, "I met a wonderful girl in Paris. She cooks, she sews, she loves housework, and she adores children," "Good," Mom commented. "We can use her on Thursdays and alternate Sundays."

*First bum: "Say, I know a rich girl who wants to get married. You can take a bath, and you can win her."

Second bum: "Yes, but suppose I take a bath and then she won't marry me, what then?"

*A prizefighter phoned his manager and said, "Look, I'm in shape. I've been in strict training. I'm ready to go. No booze. No pastries. No dames. No late hours. I'm in shape. Get me Rocky Smith. I want to fight Rocky Smith." The manager answered, "If I told you once, I told you a thousand times—you are Rocky Smith."

*The eye doctor tried patiently to please an elderly woman, trying lens after lens. Nothing seemed to be right for her.

"Now don't be discouraged," the doctor assured her. "It's not easy to get just the right glasses you know!"

"It certainly isn't," the woman replied. "Especially when you're shopping for a friend."

*A fellow walked up and down the corridor of the courthouse. Asked by an acquaintance what he was doing there, he replied, "I am a witness."

"In what trial?"

"I don't know yet. You can't tell what cases are liable to come up."

*Holding her in his arms, he gazed into her blue eyes, and whispered, "Darling, what would you do if I tried to kiss you?"

"I'd scream for father," she replied.

The young man sprang away and gulped nervously, "I thought he was out of town?"

Smiling, she whispered sweetly, "That's right. He is."

*Father: "So my daughter has consented to become your wife. Have you fixed the day of the wedding?"

Suitor: "I'll leave that to her."

Father: "Will you have a church or private wedding?"

Suitor: "Her mother can decide that, sir."

Father: "What will you have to live on?"

Suitor: "I will leave that entirely to you, sir."

*The handsome young bachelor noticed the tears in the eyes of his girlfriend. "Honey, let me kiss away those tears," he offered.

She fell into his arms, but the tears continued unabated. "Won't anything I do stop those tears?" he consoled.

"No," she answered. "It's hay fever. But please, go on with the treatment."

*"Will you marry me?" the trembling youth exclaimed, as if unable to realize his good fortune. Then "When we are

married, darling, and the dark clouds will roll away and the blue sky—"

"Just put the ring on the finger," suggested the practical-minded girl, "And you can skip the weather report."

*An office girl went into her usual self-service restaurant at her lunch hour and found all the tables taken. Finally, she sat down at a table with a very proper and dignified little old lady.

They ate silently, exchanging not a word, until the office girl finished, and lit up a cigarette. The little old lady gasped. "I'd rather commit adultery than be seen smoking in public," she said indignantly.

The office girl nodded. "Me too, but I only have an hour for lunch."

*In the middle of the Depression, the owner of a large shoe store was summoned by the vice president of the local bank. "About the loan of $200,000.00," the banker started.

The store owner held up a hand. "Mr. James," he asked, "What do you know about the shoe business?"

"Frankly," said the banker, "nothing."

"Better learn fast," advised the other. "You're in it."

*A farmer with lots of children but very little money wanted to take his family to the stock show to see a prize bull. Approaching the ticket seller, he said, "Mister, I've got a wife and fifteen children. Could you let us look at the bull for half price?"

"Fifteen children?" gasped the amazed official. "Just one minute, and I'll bring the bull to look at you."

*Little Kay was having dinner at a friend's house, and as she finished her dessert, the hostess asked, "Will you have another helping of ice cream, Kay?"

"No thank you," the girl refused politely.

"Oh, do have some more," urged the woman.

"Well, I don't know," the girl hesitated. "Mummy told me to be polite and say, 'No, thank you,' but I don't think she realized how small the first helping would be."

*A man goes to a psychiatrist and says, "Doc, my brother's crazy. He thinks he's a chicken."

The doctor says, "Why don't you turn him in?"

The guy says, "We would. But we need the eggs."

*An elephant and a mouse are talking philosophy. "Why is it," says the elephant "that although we both are God's creatures with souls of equal worth, I am huge and strong and magnificent, yet you are so tiny, puny, and gray?"

"Well," says mouse, "I've been ill, haven't I?"

*The town of Chem was known as the town of fools. One day, someone asked one of the elders which was more important—the sun or the moon.

The elders pondered the question for a long time and then replied, "The moon. The moon is more important. After all," they said, "the moon shines at night when we really need the light, while sun shines during the day when there is already plenty of light."

*Every ten years, the monks in a monastery are allowed to speak two words. Ten years go by, and it's one monk's first chance. He thinks for a second before saying, "Food bad."

Ten years later, he says, "Bed hard."

It's the big day ten years later. He gives the big monk a long, hard stare and says, "I quit."

"I am not surprised," the head monk says, "you've been complaining ever since you got here."

*Boss: "Who told you, you could neglect your office duties just because I give you a little kiss now and then?"

Secretary: "Our attorney."

*Three guys are talking about what constitutes fame.

The first guy defines it as being invited to the White House for a chat with the president.

"Nah," says the second guy. "Real fame would be if the red phone rings when you were there and the president wouldn't take the call."

"You're both wrong," says the third. "Fame is when you're in the Oval Office and the red phone rings, the president answers, listens for a second, and then says, 'It's for you.'"

*When the new patient was settled comfortably on the couch, the psychiatrist began his therapy session.

"I'm not aware of your problem," the doctor said. "So perhaps you should start at the very beginning."

"Of course," replied the patient. "In the beginning, I created the heavens and the earth."

*A man was seen dressed in exotic finery, whooping it up in the streets of a city. Someone asked him why he was doing it. "Why not?" he asked. "I am on my honeymoon."

"But where is your bride?"

"Oh she's been here before, so she stayed at home."

*So many things have been borrowed by my neighbor, I feel more at home in his house than in my own. The customer selected the socks, and when the clerk had wrapped the purchase and handed to him, the man started to leave.

"Hey, you didn't pay for those," called the clerk.

"What are you talking about?" retorted the man. "I just traded the tie for them."

"Yes, but you didn't pay for the tie."

"Why should I? Did I keep it?"

*Frank Sinatra was dining out one night, when a young high school lad came up to his table.

"Mr. Sinatra," said the teenage boy, "My name is Bernie Rosenberg. Would you please do me a favor?"

"What kind of favor?" Sinatra asked.

"Well, I'm here with my girl, and I want to make a good impression on her. I certainly would appreciate it if you would drop by my table and say, 'Hi, Bernie!'"

"OK, kid, I'll try," said the singer, smiling.

A little later, he dropped by the boy's table and said, "Hi, Bernie!"

The boy looked up at him and snapped, "Don't bother me now, Frankie. Can't you see I am busy?"

*Mrs. Ginsberg: "Thank you for a lovely party, Mrs. Liebowitz. I want you to know your brownies were so tasty. I ate four."

Mrs. Ginsberg: "Five, but who counts."

*The case of the grumpy husband:

Nothing his wife did ever made him happy. If she served him orange juice in the morning, he wanted prunes. If the toast was buttered, he wanted it plain. If the eggs were fried, he wanted them poached.

One morning, in an effort to get her husband to stop complaining, his wife cleverly fried one egg and poached the other. Then she waited for his response.

Looking at the plate, her husband grumbled, "You fried the wrong one."

*You know you are old if your walker has an air bag.

*Mary Custer: Poor Henry. Let me hold your hand.

Henry Williams: It's not heavy. I can manage.

*If God had intended man to see sunrise, he would have created it later in the day.

*A man who has to go away on a journey entrusts his daughter to a friend, requesting him to keep an eye on her virtue during his absence. After months, he comes back and discovers she has been made pregnant. Naturally, he approaches his friend. The friend alleges he cannot explain the misfortune. "Where did she sleep then?" the father finally asks.

"In my son's room."

"But how can you let her sleep in the same room with your son when I begged you to look after her?"

"But there was a screen between them. There was your daughter's bed, and there was my son's bed and the screen between them."

"And what if he'd gone round the screen?"

"I didn't think of that," said the other thoughtfully. "It could have been managed that way."

*Mr. Brown: "This is disgusting. I just found out that the janitor has made love to every woman in the building except one."

His wife: "Oh, it must be that stuck-up Mrs. Johnson on the third floor."

*One husband, for example, knew that every year on the family's way to their vacation spot, the wife would cry out, "Oh, no! I'm sure I left the iron on" to return home only to find it unplugged. One year, however, was different; the man had anticipated what was coming. When his wife gasped, "We must go back. I just know I left the iron on." He stopped the car reached under his seat and handed his wife the iron.

*"Well, Captain, I've got to admire your balls."

"Corporal Perkins!—Perhaps, later."

Religions of the World

Taoism: Shit happens.

Hinduism: This shit happened before.

Buddhism: If shit happens, it really isn't shit.

Zen: What is the sound of shit happening?

Islam: If shit happens it is the will of Allah.

Jehovah's Witness: Knock, knock, Shit happens.

Catholicism: If shit happens, I deserved it.

Judaism: Why does shit always happen to us?

(Yar Petryszyn)

*At the Union Hall, the leader stood up and spoke to the members: First the bad news. We had to settle for five percent reduction in wages. Now the good news—we managed to get it backdated six months.

*"Why are you giving me a dirty look, Mrs. Behan?"

"I didn't give you a dirty look. You had it when you came."

*The customer put five shillings on the bar counter and staggered away. Colum put it in his pocket and turned to find the accusing eye of the boss glaring at him.

"Would you believe it at all?" Colum said blandly. "He leaves five shillings tip and doesn't pay for the drink."

*Murray was muttering to himself with fiendish glee when his friend Hyland asked him what it was all about.

"I'll tell you, Hyland. That madman O'Rourke keeps slapping me on the back. Well, I've put a stick of dynamite under my coat, and this time he'll blow his arm off."

*An American tourist had been complaining a great deal about the food.

"Here," he said to the waitress holding out a piece of meat for inspection, "do you call that pig?"

"Which end of the fork sir?" she asked sweetly.

*It was three o'clock in the morning when the telephone rang beside the bed of O'Gorman, the publican.

"Mr. O'Gorman," said the alcohol-saturated voice of Cleary, "what time do you open in the morning?"

"Ten o'clock," snapped O'Gorman and hung up.

At seven o'clock, the phone rang, and it was Cleary again, "Wash time dush you open?"

"Ten o'clock but you're not going to be let in."

"I'shdon't wansh to get in. I wansh to gesh out."

*Two years ago, Doctor, I swallowed two ten-shilling pieces, and I want you to do something about them.

"Heavens, man, why didn't you come to me two years ago?"

"Sure, Doctor, I didn't need the money until now."

*"Oh, Mrs. Carey, my husband went out six months ago for a loaf of bread and never came back. What should I do?"

"Well, since you ask me, I'd say not to wait anymore. Send one of your children for another one."

*The Kerryman had a remarkable range of general knowledge, and the visitor asked him how he knew so much.

"This is the way of it," he said. "I picked a bit here and I picked up a bit there and I was too lazy to forget it."

*She followed her husband to the public house.

"How can you come here?" she said, taking a sip of his pint of stout, "and drink that awful stuff?"

"Now," he cried, "And you always said I was out enjoying myself."

*The farmer and his son were both lazy. As they sprawled in their chairs one day, the farmer said, "Paudeen, go out and see if it's raining?"

"Ah sure, can't you call the dog and see if he's wet?"

*The lecturer was proud of his ancestry, and he didn't conceal it from his County Cork audience.

"I was born an Englishman, I live as an Englishman, and I hope to die an Englishman."

"Yerra" came a loud voice from the back of the hall. "Have ye no ambition in ye at all?"

*And elsewhere, there are some people who look on insurance as a source of income rather than protection. It happened in Limerick one time.

"Clancy, my poor fella, I'm powerfully sorry to hear about your shop being burned down last Tuesday."

"Shut up, will you? That's next Tuesday."

*After each drink, Murphy took a frog from his pocket, put it on the bar counter, and stared at it.

Eventually, the barman asked him what he was up to.

"You see," said Murphy, "so long as I can see one frog, I'm sober. It's when I see two that's when I have to do something."

"And what do you do?"

"I pick up the two of them, put them in my pocket, and go home."

*A barrel maker of Kiev who had a wry sense of humor did not believe in imposing on the Lord.

"Dear God," he prayed, "all I'm asking from you is bread to eat and clothes to wear—nothing more. The schnapps, I'll buy myself."

*Tanchum, the water carrier, was returning home one evening when a stranger rushed up to him and slapped his face.

"Take that, Meyer," yelled the attacker.

Tanchum picked himself up from the street and stared at the man in amazement. Suddenly, a broad grin spread over his face and then he laughed uproariously.

"Meyer, what are you laughing at?" exclaimed the other. "I just knocked you down."

"The joke is on you," chortled Tanchum. "I'm not Meyer."

*An author who had labored for years over a book about Adolf Eichmann became so involved with the characters and unfolding events in his manuscript that it began to affect his mind. So he consulted a psychiatrist.

"Doctor," the novelist said, after he had explained his work of the past several years, "it has gotten to the point where I'm beginning to think that I myself am Eichmann. I even said so to a number of people."

"Well, don't be too concerned about it," replied the psychiatrist. "As soon as you finish the book, the delusion will disappear. After all, it isn't too serious."

"But you don't understand," protested the author. "I live in a Jewish neighborhood."

*While driving through the country, Hitler's car runs over a dog. His chauffeur stops the car, looks at the dog, and pronounces him dead. Hitler instructs the driver to inform the farmer of the accident and recompense him for the loss. The chauffeur enters the farmer's house, identifies himself, and announces, "The dog is dead."

"Wonderful," responds the farmer. "Let's drink to that good news."

*An allied soldier is shot down over Germany. He is injured and taken to the hospital.

The surgeons amputate his left leg. He asks the hospital to send his limb to his mother to be buried in US soil.

The soldier's other leg becomes infected and is also amputated. He has it sent back home for the same reason.

The infection spreads. His right arm goes and his left arm too.

He makes the same request. The hospital refuses.

"We're wise to you," the head doctor declares. "You're trying to escape."

*At a dinner debate, the French minister of finance is questioned by a student:

"M.le Ministre, how can I get into politics?"

"Where does the money in your pocket come from?" asks the Minister.

"Er . . . my father sent it to me."

"Then be assured. Once you start spending money that isn't yours, you are in politics."

*"There are," an American politician proclaimed loudly, "two things I detest above all else . . . prejudice and niggers."

*Two Germans meet on a street corner.

"Can you lend me a cigarette paper?" asks one.

"Sorry," replies the other. "I used my last one to wrap my meat ration."

*Old man to second old man.

"I like taking long walks by myself."

"Me too. Let's go."

*Two little twin boys are sent with a note, saying, "Dear Mrs. Smith, your boys say their names are Nixon and Agnew. Is this true or are they making fun of me?"

Mrs. Smith writes back, "Dear teacher, the name is Miss Smith, not Mrs. Smith, and if you had two little bastards, what would you call them?"

*Abe and his friend Sol are out for a walk together in a part of town they haven't been in. Passing a Christian church, they notice a curious sign in front, saying, "$1,000 to anyone who will convert."

"I wonder what that's about," says Abe. "I think I'll go in and have a look. I'll be back in a minute. Just wait for me."

Sol sits on a sidewalk bench and waits patiently for half an hour and then Abe reappears.

"Well," asks Sol, "what are they up to? Who are they trying to convert? Why do they care? Did you get the $1,000?"

Indignantly, Abe replies, "Money. That's all you people care about."

*She: Has there been a wedding anniversary recently?

He: Not that I remember.

She: That's what I thought.

He: You thought what?

She: That you wouldn't.

He: I wouldn't what?

She: Remember.

He: Remember what?

She: Jesus. Wedding anniversary. Wedding anniversary. That's what.

He: Oh. Thanks for reminding me. How splendid. Whose was it?

*When my grandmother was cremated, we took her ashes to Brighton.

Before she threw them off the pier, my mother forgot to check the direction of the wind.

Someone later said, "Isn't it wonderful that your mother is now in heaven."

My mother replied, "No, she's not. She's at the cleaners."

*A married couple: Although this married couple enjoyed their new fishing boat together, it was the husband who was behind the wheel operating the boat. He was concerned about what might happen in an emergency. So one day out on the lake, he said to his wife, "Please take the wheel, dear. Pretend that I am having a heart attack. You must get the boat safely to shore and dock it."

So she drove the boat to shore.

Later that evening, the wife walked into the living room where her husband was watching television. She sat down next to him, switched the TV channel, and said to him, "Please go into the kitchen, dear. Pretend I'm having a heart attack and set the table, cook dinner, and wash the dishes."

*Well, there's one thing about Sam, he's a king in his own household . . . yes, I was there the day she crowned him with a pot of beans.

*Confession: An elderly man walks into a confessional.

Man: "Father, I'm a ninety-five-year-old widower. I have many children and grandchildren, and yesterday, I went out on a date with a twenty-five-year-old super model!"

Priest: "Well, that doesn't sound like sin. You should know that as a Catholic, dating is not a sin."

Man: "Oh, I'm not a Catholic, Father, I'm Jewish."

Priest: "So why are you telling me all this?"

Man: "I'm ninety-five years old! I'm telling everybody!"

*One priest recounted the story of his first wedding, which he performed shortly after his ordination.

He had borrowed the marriage rites book, the guide containing the script of marriage ceremony, from an elderly Jesuit. The old Jesuit had written little notations in pencil because the rites book includes all of the words needed for the wedding Mass but not what you might call the "stage directions." So alongside the script for the marriage vows, the old priest had scribbled helpful directions like, "Turn to the bride," "Turn to the groom," "Go back to the presider's chair," and "Take the rings from the best man." He also wrote directions for the congregation that aren't included in the book, like saying, "Please stand" or "Please kneel."

All was going smoothly until the newly ordained priest reached the end of the vows. There was a little notation that added something that most priests say but is not included in the official Catholic rites.

The penciled-in note said, "You may now kiss the bride."

The priest found that baffling. But who was he to argue with the elderly priest who had done more weddings than he had? So the rookie priest stopped, closed his book, leaned down, and kissed the bride.

The bride stood there dumb-stuck, and everybody burst out laughing.

*Little Johnny Jones, aged seven, is in love with Mary Smith, the little girl next door, and comes to confide to his father that they plan to get married. Mr. Jones is amused. "What are you going to do for money?" he asks with pretended gravity. "I have my allowance, and Mary has nearly a dollar in the *piggy bank*." "That's all right for now," says his father, "but what will you do when the children come?" "Well, we've had pretty good luck so far."

*A professor was invited to a wedding banquet. When the time came to leave, he said to the groom, "Good luck and may you have many more."

*An Irishman went into the local bank to get a loan to buy a house. The Yankee banker looked up the record of the Irishman's bank account and then he looked over the application for the loan and then he addressed the applicant. "I have a standard test," he said. "I have one glass eye and one real eye. I'll give you the loan if you can tell me which is my glass eye and which is my real eye."

The Irishman studied each of the banker's eyes carefully. "The glass eye is the left eye," he finally said.

"You're correct," said the banker. "But how could you tell?"

"It was easy," said the Irishman. "The left eye had warmth in it."

*In 1966, at the Gridiron Dinner, Humphrey's hilarious address amply demonstrated a healthy sense of humor about himself. Describing his meeting with President Johnson just after he'd been selected as Johnson's running mate, Humphreys remembered, "President (Johnson) looked at me and said, 'Hubert, do you think you can keep your mouth shut for the next four years?' I said, 'Yes, Mr. President,' and he said, 'There you go interrupting again.'"

*People who visited the White House habitually took White House matchbooks as souvenirs. Franklin Roosevelt decided to solve this problem by imprinting on the matchbooks: "Stolen from the White House."

*Lou Cannon, the veteran reporter and Reagan biographer, recalls a fellow journalist who asked President Reagan to sign a movie photo from *Bedtime for Bonzo,* the film in which the future president starred alongside a chimpanzee. Reagan readily agreed, writing below his name, "I'm the one with the watch."

*When Edward Everett Hale served as chaplain of the Senate, he was asked, "Do you pray for the senators, Dr. Hale?"

"No," he said. "I look at the senators and pray for the country."

*When his niece expressed alarm over dinner speakers who overstepped the bounds of their allotted time, Hoover gave her some homely advice. "You just pass them up a little note saying, 'Your fly is open,' and he'll sit down right away."

*The humorist Dorothy Parker had a scathing reaction when informed of ex-President Coolidge's death in January 1933. Said Parker, "How could they tell?"

*Minutes before her husband's funeral, a widow took one last look at his body. To her horror, she saw that he was wearing a brown suit whereas she had issued strict instructions to the undertaker that she wanted him buried in a blue suit. She sought out the undertaker and demanded that the suit be changed. At first, he tried to tell her that it was too late, but when he could see she wasn't going to back down, he ordered the mortician to wheel the coffin away. A few minutes later, just as the funeral was about to start, the coffin was wheeled back in, and the corpse was now wearing a blue suit. The widow was delighted and, after the service, praised the undertaker for his swift work. "Oh, it was nothing," he said. "It so happened there was another body in the back room, and he was already dressed in a blue suit. All we had to do was switch heads."

Situational Irony (Inspired by O. Henry's Masterpiece, "The Gift of the Magi")

There was a very young couple in the bloom of spring very much in love and of very low means. They were James Danforth (Jim) and his pretty wife Della Fitzgerald (Del). They were strapped financially even after living very frugally, there was little or nothing left at the end of each month. His weekly pay was around $800, and the rent of the sparingly furnished (rent controlled) flat on the second floor on the West side of Manhattan was $200 a week.

Their cherished possessions were Del's shining, rippling cascade of long golden tresses that gently caressed her knees, and for Jim, his gold pocket watch which was given to him by his father who in turn inherited it from his father—a precious heirloom which he would ostentatiously display to Del but not to his colleagues as it did not have a fob chain which it richly deserved. He always wished to own one, but as I have said, he could not afford the luxury.

Jim worked as a copy-typist for an accounting firm Ernest and Honest and was much liked by his colleagues and superiors for his simple demeanor, polite deportment, and winning ways. He would turn up for work sharp in by the clock at eight thirty and out by the clock at four thirty. He was dependable.

Del remained in her humble abode all day. She would spend a good part of the day looking out of the window, playing mental games with what William Jennings Bryan described as the "unnumbered throng" on the street below. She never ceased to be amazed by the mix and multicultural diversity, the cross cultural collision and collusion of the American melting pot and was amused by the body language of people of different ethnic origin. That's very likely a Korean—"they are all short and stumpy" and shopping in eighty degrees, sweltering summer in sari, slippers, and bejeweled—who else but an Indian. White, pinstriped, and patent leather shoes (she smiles the two tones are things of the past) must be a banker walking across to pick up a Starbucks or "Four Bucks" as they now playfully call it. That guy taking long strides, swaying to music wired to his ears, an African American. I can see a van coming to a halt on a no-parking zone and five-stocky ones, like fire hydrants, hurriedly boarding it with pails and mops must be the Ecuadorian cleaning crew.

No, Del was by no means condescending. How could she be? She was the daughter of immigrant parents and had a ringside view of the difficult times her parents suffered through to "put food on the table." In fragmentary flashbacks, she would often recall her life with her parents. Like nostalgically reviewing an album, memories like snapshots kept returning. Parents had to walk on their heads to obtain a green card and then allowed to marinate for five tortuous years before swearing allegiance to the constitution and country. They worked seven days a week. Having had no formal education, they settled for manual work whenever and wherever they could find them. Though Christians, they never attended church. They endured grinding poverty not through couple of hours in church but by long hours of honest hard work. Sunday was their busiest day, as rich folk wanted their presence in their homes for some job or the other while they were out fishing, bowling, golfing, or whatever. The parents needed the money badly, very badly living on a day-to-day budget. As their integrity was never in question, they were in demand. Del too had become like her parents. She did not look to an external person, force, or institution for succor; rather, she looked inward and was guided by a native sense of right and wrong. Though she was a product of difficult circumstance and wore ordinary clothes picked from discounted piles from Wal-Mart or Costco—on her they were graceful. She was Dad's "precious," and he always treated her like a princess. But in times of distress, when she felt helpless, she would cry out for the mother's reassurance and comfort. It's an axiom of human existence that the umbilical cord between mother and child even if (seldom) strained is never severed.

What else did she do to fill the time until Jim returned—this young woman with a working brain and no work? You can depend on Parkinson's Law to come to your aid. "Work expands so as to fill the time available for its completion." A lady of leisure with too much time to think about the too little she had to do. With a fetish for cleanliness, she would dust and clean the apartment continuously keeping it as clean and shining as a Dutch oven. Supper was their big meal, and so she would go to great lengths to cook what Jim liked.

In the corner of the living room was a cassette player she had used as a little girl. After supper, Jim and Del would fox-trot to Frank Sinatra or Waltz to the "Beautiful Blue Danube" for a while. Thereafter, they would sit down to review the day with Del reenacting to amuse Jim with the eccentric behaviors of people she observed from the window. They lived a sedate, but by no means a sedentary life. In salubrious weather, they would take brisk walks to Central Park and there enjoy the simple joys of watching people dog walking, men and women jogging, and kids playing with parents. On their way to and from there, they would pause and window-shop. Always mindful of the other person's needs and comforts, fiercely loyal, and unconditional in their love, living in the cusp of simple Elysian happiness, it was a union that has grown to be greater than the sum of its parts.

But today was different, very different. Looking out of the window, Del was sad. Tomorrow is Christmas. She could see young and old carrying loads of Macys, Bloomingdales, and Saks. No she was not jealous. She was not that kind of a girl. She was thinking of her Jim. She always did. She had what Zadie Smith would call a "constitutional eagerness to please" her Jim at all times. "I must get something for my Jim," she says. "But then I have only five dollars, all in quarters, nickels, and dimes. I like to surprise him." *But how much surprise can I get out of five dollars*, she asked herself.

Jim and Del were only twenty-five years old, and they have been married for two years. They had the strength and sang-froid of a man and woman in the prime of life. The aura and allure of newlyweds was very much alive in the air and palpable. Jim needed new coat, shoes, and gloves. She had on many occasions suggested to Jim that she would like to look for employment to complement their meager income, but he would not hear of it. He wanted Del to look fresh and rosy as ripening fruit when he returned home from work.

I have to get something nice for Jim, she kept reminding herself. *What can I do? Where can I get the money,* she worried. And then she began to sweat profusely. She was giddy with excitement. She grabbed her coat and cap and scurried down the two flights of stairs. "Aw I forgot to close the front door." *Who cares? There's nothing there anybody wants*. She hied directly to Mme. Serioso's—"Buyer of hair goods of all shades." Panting out of sheer excitement, she rushed at Mme. Serioso with the grace of a gazelle.

"Take it easy, girl. What is it you want?" Serioso wanted to know.

Between pants, she blurted, "Will you buy my hair?"

"Remove your cap and let me see?" said Mme. Serioso.

Mme. Serioso was stunned into silence. Del's mane in all its glittering golden glory slithered down to her knees. Anyone who is willing to sacrifice to a pair of scissors such beautiful hair that must have turned many heads is desperate for the money she knew. Like a Scent-hound that had tracked his prey, Serioso was ready for the kill. Holding her excitement in check to peg the price down, with calculated indifference, she said, "Twenty dollars. Take it or leave it."

"I'll take it," said Del.

Serioso collected the sheared shock of hair into an urn as though it was something holy and put it away.

With twenty-five dollars, taking two steps at a time, she was on to the West Fifty-Fourth Street watch shop she knew very well. Pointing to the gold fob chain, she asked, "How much is that please?"

"Twenty-one dollars."

Now holding the chain and four dollars tightly in her fist, she was back at her flat. Very reluctantly, she looked at her reflection in the hand mirror and was horrified. "Serioso has skimmed away the cream. Oh what have I gone and done?" She began to rehearse. "Oh, Jim, I did this just for you. Jim, don't get mad at me. Look, Jim, what I got for you. Remember, Jim, tomorrow is Christmas." The seconds were ticking away. An eternity it seemed between seconds.

Just then, promptly as always around five, she heard footsteps up the stairs. "That's my Jim. Ma, please help me—make him understand," she sobbed. She heard the front door open.

Jim stepped inside the door and froze as Del wriggled off the table and rushed to embrace him. He simply stared at her motionless, and Del did not know what to make of it. She waited for him to say the first words.

"You have cut your hair, Del."

"And sold it just for you, Jim."

"Jim, darling please don't look at me that way," she cried. "Oh, please understand. Don't look at me that way. I had my hair cut off and sold it because I couldn't have lived through Christmas without giving you a present. I just had to do it. When you see what I've got for you, you'll forgive me. Don't be mad at me. Please, please."

Jim was not mad. Jim was not one bit mad. Jim was feeling sorry for Del. Out of his jacket pocket Jim pulled out his surprise and handed it over to Del. Del hurriedly tore open the package like a six-year-old and saw what she had always longed to own, worshipped to own, what she would drool over looking at it in a Broadway window.

There lay *the combs*—the set of combs, beautiful combs, pure tortoise shells, with bejeweled gold rims just the shade to wear in the beautiful hair that was no longer there. She ran and hugged and kissed Jim assuring repeatedly, "My hair will soon be back again, Jim. Depend on it."

Then she realized she had not given her surprise. She ran and brought her package and said, "Open it, Jim. Open it, Jim. I sold my hair to get you this. You are going to be pleased. I know it. Now you can show your watch off to your friends at office. What's holding you back?"

Jim opened the parcel and smiled. Del detected it was a painful smile—a disturbed smile. "Don't you like it, Jim? Tell me please" It pained Jim to have to disappoint Del. "I don't own a watch anymore, Del. I sold it to buy the comb. You see, Del, fate has been cunning but not cruel—tricked us both. Turned us over inside out, tested us. Showed what we truly mean to each other."

They both laughed and hugged and were filled with the joy that they gave away what was most precious to them in order to make the other happy; with tears trickling down their cheeks, humming the tune they knew only too well, they slow fox-trotted to Sinatra's, "The way you look tonight . . . Lovely, never, never change . . ."

After-Effect.

"For oft when on my couch I lie in vacant or in pensive mood"—this journey of sixteen months, may be more, from conception through consummation to creation—"will flash upon that inward eye which is the bliss of solitude" and then (with apologies to Wordsworth) "my heart will pleasure fill"

This then dear friend is my reward—no more.